GROWING IN LOVE AND WISDOM

Tibetan Buddhist Sources for
Christian Meditation

Susan J. Stabile

OXFORD
UNIVERSITY PRESS

OXFORD

UNIVERSITY PRESS

Oxford University Press is a department of the University of Oxford.
It furthers the University's objective of excellence in research,
scholarship, and education by publishing worldwide.

Oxford   New York

Auckland   Cape Town   Dar es Salaam   Hong Kong   Karachi
Kuala Lumpur   Madrid   Melbourne   Mexico City   Nairobi
New Delhi   Shanghai   Taipei   Toronto

With offices in

Argentina   Austria   Brazil   Chile   Czech Republic   France   Greece
Guatemala   Hungary   Italy   Japan   Poland   Portugal   Singapore
South Korea   Switzerland   Thailand   Turkey   Ukraine   Vietnam

Published in the United States of America by
Oxford University Press
198 Madison Avenue, New York, NY 10016

www.oup.com

Oxford is a registered trade mark of Oxford University Press
in the UK and certain other countries.

Library of Congress Cataloging-in-Publication Data
Stabile, Susan J., 1957–
Growing in love and wisdom: Tibetan Buddhist sources for
Christian meditation / Susan J. Stabile.
p. cm.
Includes bibliographical references (p.   ) and index.
ISBN 978-0-19-986262-7 (hardcover: alk. paper)
1. Buddhist meditations.   2. Christianity and other religions—Buddhism.
3. Buddhism—Relations—Christianity.   I. Title.
BQ5572.S73 2013
248.3'4—dc23   2012006973

1 3 5 7 9 8 6 4 2

Printed in the United States of America
on acid-free paper

CONTENTS

PART III
ANALYTICAL MEDITATIONS AND COMMENTARY

PART IV
OTHER MEDITATIONS AND PRACTICES

CONTENTS

GROWING IN LOVE AND WISDOM

Introduction

Some Christians may find it strange, and possibly even heretical, to adapt Buddhist prayer forms and techniques for Christian prayer. I don't.

As a Catholic Christian who spent twenty years of her adult life as a Buddhist practitioner—mainly practicing Tibetan Buddhism, but also engaging in extended periods of Theravadan Buddhist vipassana meditation—it is not surprising that my prayer life incorporates elements and techniques drawn from the Buddhist tradition. I have found that my years as a Buddhist influence my understanding of my Christianity and that much of what I learned about and experienced of Buddhist meditation during those years enriches my prayer life as a Christian. That is especially true of the analytical meditations I learned while living in Tibetan Buddhist communities in Nepal and India and continued to practice after moving back to the United States. This book reflects my desire that these meditations may serve to similarly enrich the prayer lives of others.

I have been at home in both Buddhism and Christianity and have experienced a sense of God in both. As a result, the process of adapting prayer forms and techniques from one religious tradition to another occurred quite naturally for me. Starting with my earliest retreats after I returned to Christianity in 2001, images and ideas from my Buddhist experiences arose spontaneously in my prayer. My prayer journal from one of my first eight-day directed retreats at St. Ignatius Retreat House in New York (at which I later became a member of the adjunct ministerial staff), records an experience I had of sitting under a tree picturing in my mind Thousand-Armed Chenrezig, the Buddha of compassion, who has enough hands to help whoever needs him, wherever they are. I saw Chenrezig as "one way of imaging Christ—in all places, with hands to help wherever necessary." I didn't make the connection at the time, but fans of the poetry of Gerard Manley Hopkins will recognize the congruence between my visualization and Hopkins's line in "As Kingfishers Catch Fire": "For Christ plays in ten thousand places, / Lovely in limbs, and lovely in eyes not his."[1] Later that same day I noted the usefulness of the Theravadan Buddhist vipassana approach to deal with fears and anxieties that surfaced during the retreat: "Fear and anxiety will arise, but that is no matter. This is what Jesus says. He did not promise there will not be moments when we experience pain and anxiety, but it does not matter because he is there and we can let go of these moments. This is very similar to the Buddhist idea that we cannot stop thoughts from rising but can choose whether to let them vanish or to cling to them."

In the years since that first retreat, I have come to learn that my experience is atypical, and that what has seemed so natural to me is not at all natural for many people. Instead, I have found that many people have a fear of other religions and hesitate to incorporate any elements drawn from other faith traditions into their own religious practice.

During a ten-month period in 2008–9, I presented at an Episcopal church a monthly program designed to introduce participants to the Spiritual Exercises of St. Ignatius. At the end of each meeting, I would ask for a volunteer to lead the opening prayer at our next meeting. At the end of one of our early sessions together, one of the participants volunteered to lead the following month's opening prayer, asking whether it would be acceptable to use a prayer that incorporated Tai Chi. I later learned that her intent was to use Tai Chi movements to accompany the prayer known as St. Patrick's breastplate: "Christ with me, Christ before me, Christ behind me, Christ in me..." My response was "yes, of course," pleased at this unexpected opportunity to introduce the participants to a method of praying that I was sure would be new for at least some, if not most, of them.

Within a week, however, I received a phone call from one of the other participants. My caller told me she had spoken with several other members of our group and needed to ask me how I could possibly think it was acceptable to begin one of our sessions with Tai Chi. How could we begin a gathering devoted to "Christ our King and Savior" with a practice that originated as a prayer to "Asian gods"? She spoke at length about the dangers of opening ourselves up to such outside influences, using the image of a spider's web to explain the risk she saw. We think we are on the edge of the web, she said, but really the spider (Satan) is spinning a web all around us when we engage in dangerous activities like using prayers from foreign traditions.

Apart from the fact that Tai Chi is a martial art and not a prayer practice, both my caller's reaction and its vehemence surprised me. My only personal experience with Tai Chi dated to the previous summer. At St. Ignatius Retreat House, during my annual eight-day retreat, two Catholic nuns on the retreat house's summer staff offered daily sessions of Tai Chi. The sessions were held early in the morning on the lawn outside the retreat house. I went almost every morning and I loved it. It was, for me, an experience of Hopkins's "God's Grandeur." The slow movements allowed a prayerful focus on the beauty around us and I felt both surrounded by and infused with the energy and love of God. I looked forward to the practice each morning and it was a wonderful supplement to the rest of my prayer during the retreat.

Because I believe there is only one God (albeit a Trinitarian one), the idea that a prayer could be dangerous because it was adapted from a tradition that had a different name for God was a strange one to me, as was the idea that Satan could attack us through any heartfelt prayer directed to God, regardless of its form. Nonetheless, this woman's comments opened my eyes to the fears (and the magnitude of those fears) that some people have about other faiths. I have wondered whether this kind of fear explains, for example, why the United States Conference of Catholic Bishops in 2009 condemned the practice of Reiki, a healing practice originating in Japan, as a form of superstition that corrupts the worship of God, or why many Christians (Catholic and Protestant) are suspicious of the Enneagram, a model of personality types that I have found enormously beneficial both for self-understanding and in my work as a spiritual director.

It was my recognition of the existence of this fear that first caused me to think of writing this book. My aim is to promote understanding of something that Cardinal Ratzinger (now Pope Benedict XVI) wrote in a letter to Catholic bishops in 1989, that is, that prayer and meditation practices from other religions should not be "rejected out of hand simply because they are not Christian. On the contrary, one can take from them what is useful so long as the Christian conception of prayer, its logic and requirements are never obscured."[2]

In addition to those who are afraid or suspicious of other faith traditions, there are growing numbers of individuals in the West who feel a deep spiritual hunger. This book is also addressed to them. Large numbers of Christians in the United States and Europe have looked to Buddhism and other Eastern religions for spiritual nourishment they do not perceive as available within their own faith tradition. Some have abandoned Christianity completely, but others (including many Christian monastics) have sought to incorporate some Eastern meditation practices into their Christian prayer. I hope to show the former group that they need not leave Christianity to satisfy their hunger. For the latter, this book may explore some unfamiliar territory, providing them with a new source of spiritual enrichment.

As a spiritual director and retreat director, I also hope to provide a resource for those engaged in ministry and those who train such ministers. Many of us from time to time find ourselves ministering to people of other faith traditions. Some experience outside of our own faith tradition is useful in this context. For those conducting group programs in parishes and other settings, the meditations in this book can easily be adapted to serve as guided meditations for small or large groups.

My final goal in this book is to add my voice to those trying to demonstrate that religion can be a strong force for cooperation and peace, rather than a force for division and conflict. I do not wish to naively minimize the real differences that exist among religions, which would be not only foolish, but potentially dangerous. The idea is not to reduce religion to a lowest common denominator that everyone can agree on. Rather, seeing how practices from a non-Christian faith tradition can support our own Christian practice can both lead to a deeper understanding of our own Christianity and lend a spaciousness or generosity in our approach to those who follow a non-Christian path. It may be that prayer practices and the experience of those who engage in meditation offer a more fertile common ground for promoting interfaith understanding than does a focus on doctrine.

A disclaimer is important here. This book is not a comprehensive examination or even a complete summary of the major tenets of either Tibetan Buddhism or Christianity, although, of course, it is necessary for me to talk about some major teachings of each;

that kind of study can easily be found elsewhere. Instead, my focus is on what Buddhism—more specifically, a particular form of Tibetan Buddhist meditation—has to recommend that may be helpful to a Christian who is serious about pursuing a spiritual path.

The book is divided into four parts. Part I addresses the question of how we should think about other faith traditions and why we might ever think of looking outside of our own tradition for the means to spiritual growth. The two chapters of Part II focus specifically on the idea of incorporating prayer forms that originate in a faith tradition other than our own, and in particular what Tibetan Buddhism has to offer to Christians.

There are several distinct dialogues now taking place among those interested in religion and spirituality. The two most important for the purposes of this book are the dialogue among theologians who compare and contrast the doctrines of the world's religions and the dialogue among contemplatives of different religious traditions about their respective practices and what they can learn from each other. These dialogues seem to involve entirely different casts of characters and (lamentably, in my view) do not seem to reference each other very much, if at all.

My focus is on the contemplative dialogue; what I find important in helping people deepen their relationship with God are not the doctrinal or theological differences or similarities between and among religions, but the extent to which the teachings and practices of one faith can enrich the religious practice and prayer of someone of another faith tradition. I recognize, however, that many people not already deeply rooted in a contemplative tradition cannot approach the practice without some understanding of the theological issues. Hence, my division between matters more conceptual and doctrinal in Part I and those more rooted in contemplation in Part II.

Part III of the book presents fifteen meditations for Christians adapted from Tibetan Buddhist analytical meditations, each of which is followed by a commentary. Part IV introduces some other Tibetan Buddhist meditations and practices, illuminating parallels between them and Christian practices, and suggests ways in which the former may enrich the latter. Finally, I have tried to include in the glossary any terms that might be unfamiliar to those not steeped in the Buddhist tradition.

It is not necessary to read the parts of the book in this order. For those who have some knowledge of Buddhism and are primarily interested in praxis, I would recommend proceeding directly to the meditations in Part III, which can be practiced in any order. Even those without such background might benefit from starting with the meditations and gaining some experience praying with them before returning to the earlier parts of the book. Those who feel the need to gain an intellectual understanding first will want to begin with Parts I and II. However you proceed, it is my wish and prayer that you benefit from the meditations presented here as much as I have, and that they may be a means of deepening your understanding of both Christianity and non-Christian faith traditions and, most important, your own relationship with God.

PART I

HOW WE THINK ABOUT OTHER FAITH TRADITIONS

Chapter 1

The Value of Interreligious Dialogue

People who know that I spent many years as a Buddhist before returning to Christianity often ask whether I consider myself a "Buddhist Christian" or a "Christian Buddhist." The question is understandable. Many people give themselves one or the other of those labels, just as many others self-identify as "Jewish Buddhist" or "Hindu Christian" or even as "Christian Hindu Buddhist."

Not only do I accept neither "Christian Buddhist" nor "Buddhist Christian" as an accurate label for myself, I am wary about the use of such hyphenated labels in general. My reasons for this are perhaps best understood within the context of the broader question of the value of interreligious dialogue. Why should any person of faith see any benefit in exploring other religious traditions? What is the goal of such dialogue?

Peter Phan expresses the goal of interreligious dialogue as "mutual correction and enrichment."[1] Both parties to the dialogue—both Christians and non-Christians—are invited to examine their own religious beliefs and practices with the goal of deepening their commitment to their faith and living more fully out of that commitment. For Phan, this includes the possibility that dialogue may lead to the need to correct one's beliefs and practices, something that should not frighten Christians, who understand that the church is *semper reformanda*.

This goal of mutual correction and enrichment captures well the experience of those of us who have engaged seriously with other religions. Orthodox rabbi Irving Greenberg reports of his discussions with the Dalai Lama that they taught him not only about Buddhism, but "even more about *menschlichkeit* [humanness], and most of all about Judaism." Encountering the Dalai Lama did more than reveal to him the integrity of Buddhism. "Equally valuable, the encounter reminded us of neglected aspects of ourselves, of elements in Judaism that are overlooked until they are reflected back to us in the mirror of the Other."[2] Rabbi Alan Lew writes that Zen practice helped him to discover the depth of Jewish spirituality and quotes a friend who suggested that his years of Zen meditation enabled him to understand how deep and "utterly gratifying" ordinary Jewish practices could be.[3] Tom Chetwynd made a similar observation about his experience with Zen Buddhism, explaining, "I had had the privilege to be born into Christianity, but because I had encountered Zen, I would not die in it—I would *live* in it."[4] He describes how his Zen practice allowed him to see new things in his Christian practice and "to take a fresh delight in the Mass."[5]

Brother David Steindl-Rast, a Catholic Benedictine monk from whose writings I have learned a tremendous amount, speaks of the difference between remaining rooted in a religious tradition and being stuck in it. Being rooted in our own tradition while being able to draw and learn from the truths and practices of other traditions helps the roots of our faith grow deeper. This has certainly been my experience coming back to Christianity from Buddhism; I have found that there is much in Buddhism that benefits the Christian seriously committed to deepening his or her faith and relationship with God.

During the latter part of his life, Thomas Merton, who was Catholic and a Trappist monk, became convinced that other world religions could enlighten Catholics and bring spiritual wisdom. He was fully aware that there are differences between and among religions, and he explicitly rejected syncretism and its pretense that everything from any religion can be affirmed and accepted. Nonetheless, he saw a great danger in what he termed the "heresy of individualism," a view of the self as simply "not the other," that defines the self "by negating everyone else in the universe." He warned, "If I affirm myself as Catholic merely by denying all that is Muslim, Jewish, Protestant, Hindu, Buddhist, etc., in the end I will find that there is not much left for me to affirm as a Catholic: and certainly no breath of the Spirit with which to affirm it."[6] Instead, Merton believed that the more he could say "yes" to others, the more he could discover them in himself, the more real he would be. With respect to his own faith, he believed he would be a better Catholic not by refuting all that is Protestant, but by affirming what was true in Protestantism and moving on from there. So also, he argued, for Islam, Hinduism, and Buddhism.

Merton was obviously speaking from his own standpoint as a Catholic, but his realization holds true for all Christians—there is much truth in faith traditions other than our own that we can affirm, and, to use a line I loved from the first time I heard it, any truth belongs to the Holy Spirit. Ippolito Desideri, a Christian missionary to Tibet in the eighteenth century, believed that points of convergence between two different religious traditions indirectly affirm both. Marcus Borg has made a similar observation, suggesting that "the parallels between the wisdom teaching of Jesus and the Buddha add to the credibility of both."[7]

When I talk about learning more about our own faith by encountering other faith traditions, I am talking about something that goes beyond accumulating an intellectual understanding of concepts. Rather, I am talking about an internal (as well as external) dialogue and engagement at a level that allows us to grow into a mature embrace of our own religion. Such a mature embrace occurs when the faith tradition into which you are born becomes something you freely embrace—when you call yourself Catholic, for example, not simply because your Catholic parents baptized you into that faith as a baby, but because you have committed yourself to a Catholic path, with a full understanding of what that means.

Some Christian denominations try to insulate themselves from exposure to and influence of other faiths, an approach that impedes the development of a mature spirituality; a free and knowing choice of a faith tradition is impossible absent exposure to other traditions. In an Amish tradition called Rumspringa, when Amish teens turn sixteen, they are expected to take some time (even several years) to explore the outside world before deciding to join the Amish church for life. One can question whether sixteen is too young to make this kind of determination. Nonetheless, the tradition of Rumspringa reflects the understanding that the choice to fully join the church cannot be a free one without exposure to something other than that in which the individual has been completely steeped for her entire life.

Exposure to other faith traditions also serves as a reality check. One of the tactics of religious cults is precisely to control the flow of information so that the only religious message received by members comes from the cult's leader. It is, of course, easy to say, "Well, that is true of cults, but not of my religion." (Doubtless, members of many cults would respond the same way.) But the truth remains that we need some voice outside of our own faith system to act as a check—to keep us honest so to speak, to ensure we are not being led astray.

True dialogue with other faith traditions forces us to grapple with positions that are counter to our own and to try to articulate for ourselves and others why those positions are unpersuasive, why our faith speaks a truth that another does not. Raimon Panikkar writes that "dialogue serves the useful purpose of laying bare our own assumptions and those of others, thereby giving us a more critically grounded conviction of what we hold to be true."[8] In his essay *On Liberty*, John Stuart Mill expressed the view that in matters such as morals and religions, one can arrive at truth only when one hears opposing views—and hears them "from persons who actually believe them; who defend them in earnest, and do their very utmost for them."[9]

The idea that part of the value of interreligious dialogue lies in deepening our commitment to, and enhancing our knowledge of, our own faith tradition serves to explain my approach to the question with which I opened this chapter—whether I consider myself a "Buddhist Christian" or a "Christian Buddhist."

Someone once asked the Dalai Lama if one could be a Christian and a Buddhist at the same time. The Dalai Lama said that he thought that a belief in a Creator could be associated with the understanding of the Buddhist concept of emptiness and that one could make progress along the spiritual path for some time in a way that reconciled Christian and Buddhist teachings. He believed, however, that once one reaches a certain level, a choice between the two traditions is necessary.

It is one thing to draw from another faith tradition and to examine underlying dynamics and shared values and principles that operate across faith traditions. It is another to ignore places where Christianity and Buddhism differ in fundamental respects or where they possess a shared underlying reality (although some Buddhists would likely object to my use of that phrase) yet offer different ways of expressing that shared reality.

For some people, the dual label, "Buddhist Christian" or "Christian Buddhist," may express a lack of adherence to any single tradition, a variant of the "spiritual, but not religious" approach to religion. This approach reflects a desire to pick and choose what seems valuable from different traditions while ignoring the rest. One person phrased it as finding "what works for me to keep my mind and heart peaceful, my life meaningful."[10]

As appealing as this might seem at first blush, there is a danger to the pick-and-choose approach that finds no home within any one tradition. Unmoored from a faith tradition, it is easy to fall into a "whatever feels good to me" trap that impedes serious spiritual development. This risks spirituality by whim and caprice, with no meaningful reality check on what "feels good." It may not be impossible to live an authentically holy life without being rooted in a faith tradition, but doing so is not easy.

Some who call themselves Buddhist and Christian may do so simply to convey that they draw upon both traditions in their (primary) practice of one or the other. And that is certainly something I and many others do. Nonetheless, I think such a description is potentially misleading because people are likely to understand it to imply a blending of traditions rather than an effort to use one in support of the other.

For others, it may be that the use of the label "Buddhist Christian" or "Christian Buddhist" is merely a way of recognizing that there are some important points of convergence between the two traditions. If that is the case, however, the term is too limiting because many of those points of convergence are shared by other religious traditions as well.

There also may be some who, while not necessarily calling themselves "Buddhist Christian" or "Christian Buddhist," consider themselves dual practitioners. Roger Corless, for example, viewed himself as a dual practitioner of Buddhism and Catholicism. Despite his belief that there were irreconcilable differences between the two, he found himself "convinced of the simultaneous, yet contradictory truths of Christianity and Buddhism"[11] and believed he could be present to both traditions. Similarly, Paul Knitter (who does refer to himself as a "Buddhist Christian") talks about "double-belonging," believing he "can be a Christian only by also being a Buddhist."[12] Although his primary source of identity is Christianity, Buddhism is central to Knitter's spirituality; as suggested by the title of his 2009 book—*Without Buddha I Could Not Be a Christian*—he believes he can be Christian only because of Buddhism.

"Double-belonging" doesn't fit for me. Thus, I tend to describe myself as a Christian whose Christianity is very much informed by my years as a Buddhist. It may overstate it to say I look at Christianity through a Buddhist lens, but much that I learned as a Buddhist influences how I approach Christianity.

Is there room within Christianity for the kind of interreligious dialogue whose goals and value I have articulated? The Catholic Church, in which I was raised and to which I returned after my years as a Buddhist, has spoken in a formal way on this subject, making its position on the matter useful to consider.

The Catholic Church believes itself to be the Church founded by Christ, from whom salvation comes. It, therefore, sees itself as the instrument of salvation for all of humanity, referring to itself as the "universal sacrament of salvation,"[13] possessing "the fullness of the means of salvation"[14] and the "fullest deposit of faith,"[15] a term that refers to the entirety of the revelation of Jesus Christ as passed through successive generations.

The Church does acknowledge that, through ways known only to God and not to humans, Christ may make himself known to non-Christians in a way that allows for their salvation. This is reflected in Karl Rahner's concept of the "anonymous Christian," the idea that non-Christians can accept God's grace through Christ even if they never heard of Christ; Christ and the Holy Spirit operate even where the non-Christian is not conscious of it.

Pope Pius XI is reported to have said to the Apostolic Delegate sent to Libya in 1934, "Do not think that you are going among Infidels. Muslims attain to Salvation. The ways of Providence are infinite." Similarly, in its 2000 declaration, *Dominus Iesus*, the Congregation for the Doctrine of the Faith spoke of those non-Christians who possess "a grace which, while having a mysterious relationship to the Church, does not make them formally part of the Church, but enlightens them in a way which is accommodated to their spiritual and material situation."[16] Several documents of the Second Vatican Council, most notably *Lumen Gentium* and *Nostra Aetate*, reflect Rahner's influence and contain similar expressions.

Although non-Christians can be the recipients of God's salvific grace, those who follow other faith traditions are, in the words of *Dominus Iesus*, in a "gravely deficient situation" compared to Catholics. The Church expressly and consistently rejects any form of relativism that claims that any religion is as good as any other, more specifically, that any other religion is as good as Catholicism.

Nonetheless, the Church does not reject as false everything that comes from other religions. *Nostra Aetate*, the 1965 declaration on the relation of the Catholic Church to non-Christian religions, acknowledged that there is much that is "true and holy" in the precepts and teachings of other religions and that the Church "regards with sincere reverence those ways of conduct and of life, those precepts and teachings which, though differing in many aspects from the ones she holds and sets forth, nonetheless often reflect a ray of that Truth which enlightens all men."[17]

Consistent with the spirit of *Nostra Aetate*, Pope John Paul II was a strong believer in and major promoter of interfaith dialogue, believing that "what unites us is much greater than what separates us" and that it is necessary "to rid ourselves of stereotypes, of old habits and above all, it is necessary to recognize the unity that already exists."[18] His successor, Pope Benedict XVI, has, at times, expressed less enthusiasm for interfaith dialogue, raising a suspicion that interreligious dialogue requires "setting one's faith aside" (a phrase taken from a letter he wrote in 2008 to Italian philosopher Marcello Pera)[19] and opens the door to relativism.

If the aim of interreligious dialogue were a syncretism that truly required individuals to set aside their own beliefs in search of some kind of lowest common denominator or that sought the homogenization of all religions into one, concerns about setting aside one's faith would be legitimate. The goal, however, is not to suggest that all religions are the same or to shy away from discussions of their differences. Nor is it to try to remake other religions into our own. Rather, the aim is to find those areas in which we can learn from each other in a way that allows us to deepen our own faith, as well as to better understand which differences among religions reflect different core principles and foundational truths and which are merely different ways of expressing the same core principles and foundational truths.

It is certainly true that if you take the position that your own faith tradition has nothing to learn from another faith tradition, even this goal seems suspect. In the case of Catholicism, the traditional Catholic view of itself as having the fullest "deposit of faith" is too easily (and mistakenly) translated into precisely that attitude, one that I have heard expressed by more than one Catholic. If you think it is misguided or "gravely deficient" to follow another religion, it is easy to assume that you should avoid (and perhaps even fear) anything coming out of another faith tradition.

This is much less troubling to many Buddhists, particularly Tibetan Buddhists, who tend to view the existence of different religions as reflective of both different cultural influences and the fact that individuals have different inclinations, abilities, and interests. Notwithstanding the expansive spread of Buddhism beyond the place of its birth and the large number of Westerners who flock to Buddhist teachers, Tibetan Buddhists today don't actively seek to convert others to Buddhism. The Dalai Lama has explicitly said that conversion "is not the point," that "humanity needs all the world's religions to suit the ways of life, diverse spiritual needs, and inherited national traditions of individual human beings."[20] On more than one occasion he has said that it is better not to convert from one religion to another, believing it to be generally better for people to stay within their own religious tradition and culture. Similarly, the late Chogyam Trungpa Rinpoche once told a Jewish student of his that he should observe the Jewish Sabbath as his meditation practice.[21] Similar sentiments have been expressed by Hindu teachers. One Hindu teacher reportedly responded to a Christian who told him he planned to convert to Hinduism, "If you think you should convert, then you insult both your religion and Hinduism."[22]

It is also the case that many Buddhists hold less tightly to doctrine than do Christians, eschewing attachment to anything, even to ideology. The first of Thich Nhat Hanh's *Fourteen Precepts of Engaged Buddhism* is a determination "not be idolatrous about or bound to any doctrine, theory, or ideology, even Buddhist ones. Buddhist systems of thought are guiding means; they are not absolute truth."[23] It may thus be easier for many Buddhists to approach interfaith dialogue in a more open and positive way than is possible for at least some Christians.

I am hopeful that even those Christians with doubts as to whether other traditions have anything to teach them will be willing to entertain the possibility that there might be something in what I present here for them. I leave the question of what Buddhists can learn from Christians for another project.

Chapter 2

Core Truths That Operate Across Faith Traditions

In his introduction to a book edited by Marcus Borg titled *Jesus and Buddha: The Parallel Sayings*, Jack Kornfield writes about having been taken some years ago to see two statues that stand on the shore of an island in Vietnam. One is an image of the Buddha and the other is Jesus. The two figures stand with "their arms around each other's shoulders, smiling." With the war raging around them, Kornfield observes, "Buddha and Jesus stood there like brothers, expressing compassion and healing for all who would follow their way." These statues, he wrote, expressed a "bond of love [that] rests on the universal wisdom that they share."[1]

It is incontrovertible that the faith traditions of the world share many common values and understandings, and some wonderful recent books have explored those commonalities, notably His Holiness the Dalai Lama's *Toward a True Kinship of Faith: How the World's Religions Can Come Together*, and Brother David Steindl-Rast's *Deeper Than Words: Living the Apostles' Creed*.

That there are such common values and understandings is not to say, as some people do, that all religions are the same or that all religions are one. There would be little need to discuss religious tolerance if there were not differences among religions. What is there for you to tolerate, after all, unless there is another group who holds views you think are mistaken (i.e., different from your own views) in some significant respect? There is no benefit in ignoring the real differences between Buddhism and Christianity (and among the other major world religions). On this point I agree both with Stephen Prothero, who argues that pretending there is no difference among religions, like all forms of ignorance, makes the world a more dangerous place, and with Pope Benedict, who suggests that the quest to discover commonalities among religions risks tempting us to shy away from frankly discussing differences for the sake of harmony.

Notwithstanding the differences, however, there are also points of real convergence, and there are truths to be found in religions other than our own. Even *Dominus Iesus* acknowledges that "the various religious traditions contain and offer religious elements which come from God."[2]

For a Christian, the idea of a religion not explicitly centered on God may seem strange or difficult. Nonetheless, on some fairly fundamental matters Buddha and Jesus Christ use virtually the same language as they invite their followers to embark on a new path and a fundamental transformation.

In exploring points of convergence between Buddhism and Christianity, it is particularly important to be attentive to the fact that some things that are perceived as differences between the two amount to little more than different words for similar concepts or different ways of expressing the same underlying reality. Stephen Prothero argues, for example, that major world religions address fundamentally different problems, claiming that Buddhism and Christianity are concerned, respectively, with the suffering of cyclic existence, (i.e., the cycle of birth and rebirth we experience, *samsara* in Sanskrit) and with sin as the basic human problem. It is true that Buddhists don't speak of sin and Christians don't speak of cyclic existence. However, both religions recognize the same fundamental human drives and "delusions." The delusions that

Buddhists believe keep humans in the suffering cycle of birth and rebirth are no different from those that, in Christian terms, cause alienation from God (sin).

In this chapter I explore some of the underlying dynamics and shared values and principles that operate across faith traditions as a way to help explain why I believe Christians can profit from prayer practices that come from outside of their own faith tradition. These shared values and principles underlie the meditations I present in Part III. Although I examine these dynamics separately, you will see a great deal of overlap among them.

At the outset, let me acknowledge that Christianity is not a monolith. There are many different denominations of Christianity and they differ in their views on any number of issues. The core issues I discuss here, however, are broadly accepted by all who call themselves Christians.

RELATIONSHIP TO THE PHYSICAL WORLD: IMPERMANENCE AND RENUNCIATION

Religion implies an acceptance of transcendence, of life beyond our ordinary range of perception, of something beyond ourselves and this world. The Dalai Lama put it well when he said that "at the heart of all the world's religions is a vision of human life that transcends the boundaries of an individual's physical existence as an embodied, finite, and temporal being. A meaningful life, in all the faith traditions, is one that is lived with an awareness of a supra-mundane dimension."[3]

At the level of our everyday reality, it is easy to lose that awareness and to be consumed by this world. We can easily become wrapped up in our need to earn a living and to perform the daily tasks necessary to sustain our existence. We tend, in the ordinary course of events, to think of "life" as beginning with our human birth and ending with our human death.

If we are spiritual people, however, we know that we are defined by more than our human existence. We understand that this current human existence of ours is a blip in the totality of life eternal. We are temporary visitors to this planet, as one of my Jesuit friends describes it. Nonetheless, we don't tend to behave as though we were temporary visitors—our everyday selves view the physical world we inhabit as our "life." That is, after all (except for those who claim to have memories of past lives), the only life we know.

The idea of *impermanence* captures this reality, that all things in this world are transitory. This is one of the most basic insights of Buddhism, the idea that all of reality is constantly changing. From moment to moment, nothing remains stable, nothing is permanent. Our bodies, thoughts, feelings, and all the things of this world are continually in an ongoing process of change.

Some changes are readily apparent. My daughter today looks visibly different from the way she did a year ago. The weather in Minneapolis, where I currently live, feels very different in January than it feels in June.

Other changes, however, are much more subtle and not as easily perceived. For example, when we look at a table or a chair, we see a permanent, static object—we see table or chair. I walk downstairs in the morning and, to my perception, I sit on the same stool that was in my kitchen when I went upstairs to bed the night before. Buddhism explains, however, that what we see as a static, unchanging, and solid object is, in fact, just a series of causally related processes. Think of the way movies were made in a predigital age. What we saw was action, but what was really before our eyes was a series of still pictures running rapidly through the projector so as to give the illusion of action and movement.

The stool I sit on at breakfast is not only different from the stool I sat on the night before, it is not the same as the stool that existed a moment before I sat down on it. In Buddhist thought, nothing—not objects, people, thoughts, feelings—is permanent. Everything changes moment by moment.

Buddhism explains that we are habituated not to see impermanence and thus live under an illusion—the illusion of permanence. We come to believe that things possess a constancy that they lack. This illusion creates frustration and insecurity as we continually try to grasp at things that are not there. Part of the aim of the Buddhist path is to develop a realization of the impermanent nature of things and to integrate that realization into our lives.

Christians do not use the term "impermanence" the way that Buddhists do. However, Christianity does have a conception of the transience of the things of this world.

In the First Letter to the Corinthians, Paul says, "if there are gifts of prophecy, they will be done away; if there are tongues, they will cease; if there is knowledge, it will be done away. For we know in part and we prophesy in part; but when the perfect comes, the partial will be done away" (1 Cor 13:8–10).

In Luke, Jesus says, "Heaven and earth will pass away, but My words will not pass away" (Lk 21:33).

Pope Benedict spoke of both the melancholy and the consolation of the transiency of the things of this world in a reflection at the end of 2009. The passing away of things that weigh us down and cause us distress gives us the peace and confidence to deal with our ongoing struggles, secure in the knowledge that "these too will pass." The flip side of this consoling thought is that *nothing* "that is within time" lasts. Along with the difficulties we have faced, "much that is beautiful has passed away, and the more we move beyond the midpoint of our lives, the more poignantly we feel this change of what was once future and then present into something past."[4]

Archbishop of Canterbury Rowan Williams expresses the Christian understanding of God's action in the universe in words that sound very close to the way Buddhism talks about impermanence. He describes creation as "an action of God that sets up a relationship between God and what is not God." The world created by God, he writes, "depends on him moment by moment, carried along on the current of his activity.... We may look at something that seems unmoving and unchanging, like the pillars of a cathedral or the peaks of a mountain, but what is within and beyond it is an intense energy and movement."[5]

Impermanence entails a view about the relationship of the individual to the world that is captured in the idea of *renunciation*, a term that is easily misunderstood. Renunciation sounds very negative to us. We hear the word and we cringe, thinking it means we are being asked to completely give things up, or at least that we are not supposed to enjoy them.

Properly understood, however, renunciation is not at all about not enjoying what we have. Rather, renunciation means living with an understanding that impermanent worldly pleasures can never be enough for us, that they are too trivial to satisfy our total nature. It is an acknowledgment that our life holds more than what we currently experience and that we need more than transitory worldly pleasures. To be truly happy requires a transformation from materialism to a life of spirit.

Most people believe that the source of happiness is external—that attaining the object of their desire (a person, an object, a house, or a job) will bring happiness—indeed, that it will bring some permanent happiness. From a Buddhist perspective, however, not only can none of these things give eternal and perfect happiness, but it is the very attachment to such things—the craving and clinging to them—that causes suffering. Lama Yeshe, who did much to bring Tibetan Buddhism to Westerners, wrote, "Contrary to what some people might believe, there is nothing wrong with having pleasures and enjoyments. What *is* wrong is the confused way we grasp onto those pleasures, turning them from a source of happiness into a source of pain and dissatisfaction. It is such grasping and attachment that is the problem, not the pleasures themselves."[6]

Renunciation is the mind-set that understands that the principal cause of happiness is not external to us but rather lies in the mind. Once we understand that, we are able to let go of attachments to the external things of this world. This is reflected in the Four Noble Truths of Buddhism: the first recognizes that our existence is characterized by suffering, by which Buddhists mean the unsatisfactory nature of all human experience; the second names clinging and grasping as the cause of suffering; the third recognizes that cessation of suffering is possible; and the fourth identifies the means of bringing about the cessation of suffering. Only by developing a deep realization that everything is impermanent and cannot bring lasting peace can we find the path to the cessation of suffering.

Although it is not expressed in identical terms, the idea of renunciation is also found in Christian scripture. Jesus directly says: "No one can serve two masters; for either he will hate the one and love the other, or he will be devoted to the one and despise the other. You cannot serve God and wealth" (Mt 6:24). Similarly, Jesus tells the rich young man who asks what he must do to inherit eternal life, "sell your possessions and give to the poor, and you will have treasure in heaven; and come, follow Me" (Mt 19:21). Most commentators do not read Jesus as literally meaning that we have to relinquish all of our possessions in order to attain salvation. Rather, he is talking about having a proper relationship to the things of this world, one that does not let our attachment and desire for such things displace the centrality of God and our service to God in the world.

The Hindu religion speaks of renunciation in terms that make clear that it is not something negative, but a signal that life holds more than we are now experiencing. What people ultimately desire, Hindus believe, is liberation (*moksha*)—release from the false sense of individuality that prevents us from attaining union with God.

The expressed goal of renunciation is not quite the same across faith traditions. In Christianity, we seek detachment from the things of this world so that we may more fully give ourselves over to God. For Christians, renunciation is about the ability to make a complete self-offering to God, recognizing that we need nothing other than God's love. For Buddhists and Hindus, it would be more accurate to say that renunciation and detachment are about giving up those things that interfere with spiritual development. The goal is to be freed to reach a higher spiritual state.

I want to underscore this point: renunciation is not about the external things we have or don't have, but about the state of our mind. We can enjoy things in this world with an attitude of renunciation just as we may lack the things of this world while still clinging to them. That means that we cannot judge another person's level of renunciation merely by appearance, which tells us nothing about the person's state of mind. "Beggars and street dogs," Lama Thubten Zopa Rinpoche writes, "eat poor food, but this does not mean they have renounced this life.... You may look renounced because you wear ragged clothes and eat poor food, but your mind may be strongly craving a reputation."[7]

When I first read Lama Zopa's words, what immediately came to mind was a passage in Thomas Merton's *Conjectures of a Guilty Bystander*. Talking about what it meant to leave the world when he entered the monastery, Merton explained that what he abandoned was a set of standards and an image of what made people happy, rather than things themselves. Without the internal change, monasticism would be "simply a fancy-dress adaptation of what we are claiming we have renounced." Merton is almost derisive in dismissing the notion that "'leaving the world' [could be] adequately summed up by those pictures of 'the Trappist' with his cowl over his head and his back to the camera, looking at the lake."[8]

Lama Yeshe taught that there is no reason at all to feel guilty about enjoying things and, in fact, that feeling guilt is "just as mistaken as grasping onto passing pleasures."[9] Renunciation doesn't mean you can't enjoy your ice-cream cone when you have it; what it means is that you don't walk around thinking, "I have to have an ice-cream cone. I need the ice-cream cone." It is not the item that is condemned; it is the attachment to it—the sense that you have to have it to be happy. Similarly, Cardinal Ratzinger wrote that "the emptiness which God requires [is] that of the renunciation of personal selfishness, not necessarily that of the renunciation of those created things which he has given us and among which he has placed us."[10]

In the words of Lama Yeshe, if we can teach ourselves to "experience happiness without the polluted attitudes of either grasping attachment or guilt, we can cultivate deeper and deeper levels of this experience and eventually attain the inconceivable happiness of our full human potential."[11] Sounds a bit like the Christian idea of losing our life in order to gain it.

Impermanence also implies recognizing that our finite lives do not have a fixed term and that death can come at any time. A meaningful understanding that death may occur in any moment entails something more than intellectual assent. It is easy to say, "Of course I know that I can die at any time. Who doesn't know that?" But the truth is that we don't live that way. Instead, we live, in the words of Lama Thubten Zopa Rinpoche, with "the hallucination that this life will last a long time, that having a human body, friends, comforts, and enjoyment will last."[12]

Jesus told more than one parable meant to teach his followers that our life span is uncertain and that we must live our lives meaningfully in the time we have. In the parable of the servants who await their master's return from a wedding, Jesus warns that "if the head of the house had known at what hour the thief was coming, he would not have allowed his house be broken into" (Lk 12:39). Explaining the parable to Peter, Jesus observes that the "servant's master will come on an unexpected day and at an unknown hour" (Lk 12:46). In another parable the rich man whose response to his bountiful harvest was to tear down his barns and build bigger barns so as to have "many goods laid up for many years to come" learns that "this very night your soul is required of you; and now who will own the things you have prepared?" (Lk 12:19–20). This story could have been written by the Buddha, who in the Udanavarga taught that "it is the law of humanity that though one accumulates hundreds of thousands of worldly goods, one still succumbs to the spell of death. All hoarding will be dispersed, whatever rises will be cast down, all meetings must end in separation, life must finally end in death" (Udanavarga 1:20–22).

The purpose of thinking about death is not to make us glum or depressed. Instead, the realization that death can occur at any moment spurs us to use our time wisely. For both Christians and Buddhists "wisely" implies something other than concern for success as defined by the secular world. For Christians it means deepening our relationship with God and preaching the Gospel by our words and deeds, preparing ourselves for ultimate union with God. For Buddhists, it means working to attain Enlightenment.

RELATIONSHIP TO ONE ANOTHER: SHARED VALUES OF COMPASSION, GENEROSITY, AND FORGIVENESS

Christianity and Buddhism share a fundamental set of values having to do with relationships between and among human beings. Among those shared values are compassion, generosity, and forgiveness.

Compassion, or a love and cherishing of others, sometimes described as a universal, nondiscriminating love, is perhaps the most widely shared value among the world's major religions.

Love is the central Christian commandment. Christ commanded his disciples to "love one another, even as I have loved you" (Jn 13:34). He did not mean by "love" the sweet emotion we feel toward those who are good to us. Rather, he taught an agapic love that is universal and that desires the well-being of the other regardless of his or her behavior toward us. This is implicit in his command that we love not only our friends, but also our enemies.

Christian love of others also means not viewing our own needs and desires as more important than those of others. That means not only not choosing the self over others, but choosing the good of others over the good of the self. Christianity teaches, "with humility of mind regard one another as more important than yourselves; do not merely look out for your own personal interests, but also for the interests of others" (Phil 2:3–4).

For Christians, Jesus is the supreme model of compassion and cherishing others over the self. His acts of healing stemmed from his compassion. "He saw a large crowd, and felt compassion for them and healed their sick" (Mt 14:14). When he met the funeral procession of a mother's only son, "He felt compassion for her.... And He said, 'Young man, I say to you, arise!'" (Lk 7:13–14). By accepting death Jesus committed the ultimate act of self-sacrifice, and he was explicit that his behavior was intended as a model for our own. In John's Gospel, Jesus amplifies the command to "love one another, just as I have loved you" with the statement that "Greater love has no one than this, that one lay down his life for his friends" (Jn 15:12–13).

The same emphasis on universal compassion is found in Buddhism. "The bodhisattva loves all living beings as if each were his only child," says the Buddha in the Vimalakirtinirdesha Sutra. In words that call to mind Isaiah's comparison of God's love to that of a mother, the Buddha in the Sutta Nipata teaches, "Just as a mother would protect her only child at the risk of her own life, even so, cultivate a boundless heart toward all beings. Let your thoughts of boundless love pervade the whole world." The Dalai Lama talks about compassion in the same way that Christians understand agapic love, distinguishing it from love that is based on attachment. Real love, he says, is not based on attachment, but is undiscriminating, spontaneous, and unlimited.

In the Itivuttaka, the Buddha taught: "Whatever grounds there are for making merit productive of a future birth, all these do not equal a sixteenth part of the mind-release of loving-kindness. The mind-release of loving-kindness surpasses them and shines forth, bright and brilliant." That doesn't sound all that different from Paul's First Letter to the Corinthians, in which he writes, "If I speak with the tongues of men and of angels...if I have the gift of prophecy, and know all mysteries and all knowledge; and if I have all faith, so as to remove mountains, but do not have love, I am nothing" (1 Cor 13:1–2). Indeed, a teaching of Lama Thubten Zopa Rinpoche on compassion echoes Paul's series of "even ifs"—even if you are a Buddhist...even if you know all the teachings...even if you have extensive intellectual understanding...even if you have many diamonds or dollars, if you lack compassion, "your life is empty."[13]

Jesus' teachings on loving one's enemies are also paralleled in the words of the Buddha. The Buddha spoke of "Considering others as yourself" (Dhammapada 10.1) and taught that "Hatreds do not ever cease in this world by hating, but by not hating; this is an eternal truth.... Overcome anger by nonanger, overcome evil by good" (Dhammapada 1.5).

The Dalai Lama refers to compassion as a fundamental spiritual value, indeed, as the highest possible spiritual value. He identifies "the compassionate ideal of relieving others from suffering" as central to both Buddhism and Christianity, and describes Christ's crucifixion as a "self-sacrifice, born out of altruism and universal love for all beings" that is a "perfect example of what Buddhists might term the Bodhisattva ideal."[14]

For both Christians and Buddhists, this universal compassion translates into a motivation to labor for the welfare of others. The highest motivation possible for a Mahayana Buddhist is the desire to achieve enlightenment, not for an individual's own sake, but for the sake of helping to relieve others from their suffering. As one lama expressed it, seeing that others suffer just as we suffer must move us to action: "I should try to do something for them and the ultimate solution, the best of all would be for me to become a fully enlightened Buddha so that I will be able to work continuously, effortlessly for the benefit of all."[15]

Thus, as Christ commands us to love even our enemies, Buddhists seek to develop a desire to help all beings without distinction—to cherish all others over the self, without regard to how they behave toward us. The goals may be characterized differently—Christians are called to labor with Christ to manifest God's Kingdom, and Buddhists seek to attain Enlightenment for the sake of all sentient beings—but Christians and Buddhists are united in seeing that love implies a commitment to active service on behalf of others. Spirituality and spiritual growth can never solely be about me and God (or only about the self, in Buddhist terms) but must include relationship to others and work done on their behalf.

Compassion is also a fundamental value in Judaism. The Torah teaches that we should love our neighbor as we love ourselves. The Mishnah, a major work of Rabbinic Judaism, makes clear that such love includes a willingness to sacrifice one's life and possessions if necessary. Likewise, compassion is the first of the "Three Treasures of Taoism," and is also an important concept in Islam. In a teaching on "Practicing the Good Heart," Lama Thubten Zopa Rinpoche observed, "I think the fundamental practice of all religions, not only of Buddhism, is to abandon giving harm to others, and to practice compassion. This is the essence of all the various religions: [Islam], Christianity, Hinduism. The essence is not giving harm to others, and generating compassion towards them."[16]

Universal compassion does not mean we won't feel closer to some people than to others. Agapic love does not mean I will like everyone equally or that I won't prefer to spend my free time with some people rather than others. Pope Benedict (while he was still Joseph Ratzinger) distinguished between agapic and brotherly love, suggesting that while agapic love—the universal love and compassion of which I have been speaking—is appropriately extended toward all people, there is a brotherly love that is appropriately directed only toward other Christians.

Flowing from a common emphasis on compassion are two other values shared by Buddhists and Christians: *generosity* and *forgiveness*. From a Christian perspective we cannot say we love God if we are not generous in providing for the needs of our brothers and sisters. In Matthew's Gospel (Mt 25) Jesus tells his disciples that when they feed the hungry and clothe the naked, they feed and clothe him and that the failure to do so is a sin against God. The Letter to the Romans encourages "contributing to the needs of the saints, practicing hospitality" (Rom 12:13).

Generosity has the same importance in the Buddhist tradition. Generosity was one of the first practices the Buddha taught to laypeople, telling them, "The wise one, however, rejoicing in charity, becomes thereby happy in the beyond" (Dhammapada 13.11). In Tibetan Buddhism, generosity is one of the so-called Six Perfections. There generosity is the mind that is happy to give to others in every way. The practice of generosity involves giving time and energy, not just goods, and also involves giving freely to all, whether you like them or not.

Both Christianity and Buddhism see generosity as something that flows naturally from a heart that loves others and that abandons a selfish concern for our own happiness. And for both, giving up a selfish concern for our own happiness is paradoxically the route to greater happiness and avoidance of suffering. For neither Christians nor Buddhists, however, is generosity only an expression of compassion. Rather, generosity creates a great freedom that allows for our spiritual growth. When Jesus told the rich young man to sell all he had and give it to the poor, his message had as much to do with ridding ourselves of those things that keep us from wholeheartedly committing ourselves to God, as with actually selling our possessions. Likewise, from a Buddhist perspective, generosity opens our heart, disposing us to the attainment of insight. The state of mind of the generous giver, referred to as *caga*, functions as an aid to meditation.

Generosity is a value in other faiths as well. The Hebrew scriptures repeatedly affirm the importance of having a generous heart. A Hindu proverb teaches, "They who give have all things. They who withhold have nothing," which is virtually identical with the

Taoist saying: "The wise man does not lay up his own treasures. The more he gives to others, the more he has for his own." Mohammad, the prophet of Islam, urged the miserly to be more generous and charitable.

Although some might think that generosity is a nice-thing-to-do-if-we-feel-like-it practice, something for which we should get a pat on the back, it is more appropriately viewed as a moral obligation. Working for the benefit of others is not above and beyond the call of duty; it is our duty. Judaism imposes an obligation of Tzedakah, giving aid and assistance to the poor and needy. Almsgiving is also one of the Five Pillars of Islam.

Also flowing from a common emphasis on compassion is *forgiveness*. Jesus spoke frequently on the subject of forgiveness, both indirectly and directly—as when he taught his disciples to ask God to forgive us our trespasses as we forgive those who trespass against us. Jesus warned against making offerings at the altar without first becoming reconciled with a brother with whom we are on bad terms (Mt 5:23–34). When Peter asked if he had to forgive someone who sinned against him as many as seven times, Jesus said, not seven, but up to seventy times seven (Mt 18:21–22). Perhaps Jesus' best-known teachings on forgiveness are his parables of the unforgiving servant (Mt 18:23–35) and of the prodigal son (Lk 15:11–32), designed both to help us appreciate the extent of God's forgiveness of our failings and to encourage our forgiveness of each other. The ultimate Christian model for forgiveness is Jesus on the cross, asking God to forgive those who had crucified him.

There is a similar emphasis on forgiveness in Buddhism. The Buddha taught that if someone should give you a blow with his hand, with a stick, or with a knife, you should abandon any desire and speak no evil words against him. In his *Bodhisattvacharyavatara* (*A Guide to the Bodhisattva's Way of Life*), Shantideva devotes many paragraphs to explaining why we should abandon any form of anger or bad feeling toward those who wrong us. The Buddhist admonition is always to practice loving kindness and forgiveness, recognizing that those who harm us are the victims of their delusions.

Other faiths similarly views forgiveness as a great power and virtue. The Hindu Mahabharata asks rhetorically, "What is there that forgiveness cannot achieve? What can a wicked person do unto him who carries the sabre of forgiveness in his hand?"[17] The Qur'an makes clear that the true believers are those who not only avoid sin and vice, but those who forgive when angered, and that God rewards those who do so. Judaism requires the individual to grant forgiveness to anyone who seeks it.

It is not only the values of compassion, generosity, and forgiveness themselves that are shared by Buddhism and Christianity. The two traditions also share an understanding of interdependence that helps ground these values, a deep realization of which makes adherence to the values flow more naturally.

Christianity views the human person as communal and interrelated. Human life is fulfilled in communion with others and with God. Created in the image of a Triune God, human beings exist in relationship both to God, as Creator—who continually breathes life into each of us—and to all other human beings. The intimacy of our relationship with God is expressed repeatedly in the Christian scriptures, as when Christ told his disciples, "I am in my Father, and you in me, and I in you" (Jn 14:20). Similar expressions can be found in the revelatory experience of persons of prayer. If you read any of the great mystics of the Christian tradition, you are familiar with their descriptions of their contemplative experience of union with God and others.

As we are one with God, so we are one with each other, since all share this relationship with God. As St. Paul told the Romans, "we, who are many, are one body in Christ, and individually members one of another" (Rom 12:5). Speaking to pilgrims in St. Peter's Square, Pope John Paul II once said that "God is not solitude but perfect communion.... From God, who is communion, derives the vocation of the whole of humanity to form one great family."[18] It is for this reason that loving others and loving God are intimately linked.

This Christian view of interrelatedness is in stark contrast to a secular vision of the human person—of individuals as self-existent and separate from others. Under that vision, the individual is not only viewed as independent and separate from others, but to the extent that the existence of God or some other Ultimate Reality is acknowledged, the individual is viewed as separate from that God or that other Ultimate Reality. Richard Garnett has suggested that our society has "embraced an account in which the person is and should be regarded as un-tethered, unsituated, and alone. He is 'autonomous,' not simply in the obvious sense that his choices are not determined or crudely reducible, but in that the only standards against which those choices can be evaluated and judged are those that he generates or endorses."[19]

This leads to a view of individuals as motivated solely or primarily by self-interest. It is this kind of view that led Adam Smith to observe 250 years ago, "It is not from the benevolence of the butcher, the brewer or the baker that we expect our dinner, but from their regard to their own self-interest. We address ourselves, not to their humanity but to their self-love, and never talk to them of our own necessities but of their advantages."[20]

It is easy to see how the Christian view leads to the promotion of values such as compassion and cherishing of others, generosity, and forgiveness. To cherish others over the self—and the attitudes that flow from that—is a hard teaching if we see an absolute division between ourselves and others. However, it is a much easier teaching once we cease to view others as completely unrelated to ourselves. Once we see our fundamental interdependence, what we now think of as altruism, concerning the true occurrence of which many are suspicious, is not really altruism at all, but an act to the benefit of the one communal body of which the actor is a part.

Buddhists also view interdependence as a fundamental law of nature. The Dalai Lama explains that all beings—from the smallest insects to the highest forms of life—have an innate recognition of their interconnectedness. The same is true for all material phenomena. "All phenomena," he writes, "from the planet we inhabit to the oceans, clouds, forests and flowers that surround us, arise in dependence upon subtle patterns of energy. Without their proper interaction, they dissolve and decay."[21] Similarly, Zen Buddhism speaks of everyone being part of one mind, much the way a Christian might think of all humans being part of one Body of Christ.

The Dalai Lama has further explained that the recognition of the interrelationship between self and others, along with the understanding that all beings are equal in their desire for happiness and to avoid suffering, is what grounds Buddhist compassion.[22] When we are not aware that we are part of an interconnected whole, we act in ways that protect our ego—often to the detriment of others.

In both Buddhism and Christianity, there are what Buddhists might refer to as lower levels of motivation for compassion, generosity, and forgiveness. In Christian terms this might be a desire to avoid the punishment of hell that is the consequence of sinful behavior. A Buddhist would refer to it as a desire to avoid negative karma or an unfortunate rebirth flowing from bad behavior. In both cases the "higher motivation" flows from the recognition of interdependence and oneness—with each other and with the interconnected whole for Buddhists, and with each other and God for Christians.

Other world religions speak of interrelationship as well. Confucianism has a strong sense of the interdependence of all people and things. The self is viewed as existing in relation to a network that begins with family and then community and extends out to encompass the world. The Confucian idea that people can become fully human only in community is very close to a Catholic understanding of the human person. Jewish wisdom teaches that divine existence engenders the existence of all of creation, and that there is nothing—not even the tiniest thing—that is not part of this connectedness. Martin Buber described Hasidism as embracing "the whole of life as a unity.... all is one kingdom, one spirit, one reality" and suggested that fulfillment is possible only in true community, in the "unity of the human community in the sight of God."[23]

There is, however, a major difference between the Buddhist and Christian understandings of interdependence. For Buddhists, nothing exists other than in interdependence on all other things; there is no creator God who transcends the things of the world. For Christians, God does not exist in dependence on anything. We live completely in dependence on God, but God is completely independent of cause and condition.

Buddhism is also more explicit than Christianity with respect to the basis for our perception that the self exists independently of others. Buddhism sees the belief in an individual self-existent person as the product of illusion. From birth, the ignorant mind has a concept of "I" as self-existent. The sense of "I," of separate existence, grows stronger and gives rise to a sense of other. The dichotomy between self and other gives rise to a sense of the importance of the self. The effort to protect the self leads us further to divide things into categories based on how they affect the ego:

things become good or beautiful because they please the ego and the ego develops attachment for such things; things are labeled bad or ugly because they increase the ego's fear and insecurity and the ego develops an aversion to such things.

According to the concept of emptiness, there is no self that exists as an unconditioned and self-existent entity. Emptiness or no-self is not nihilist; it does not assert that nothing exists. As Lama Zopa Rinpoche once said, if you fall into a fire and start to burn, it doesn't help to think, "There is no fire." Emptiness does not mean nonexistence, but rather that everything exists "as a dependent arising" in relation to other things. Lama Yeshe described the *shunyata* or emptiness mantra as expressing: "All existent phenomena in the universe and I are of one reality."[24] The Dalai Lama speaks of emptiness as "the truth of the profound interdependent nature of all things."[25]

From a Buddhist perspective, the illusion of self and independence stems from the distractions, false assumptions, and self-regarding instincts that make up our surface selves. The goal is to break that illusion, to see things as they really are. At the level of practice, *bodhicitta*—the mind that cherishes others over the self—is not viewed as completely distinct from the realization of emptiness. Bodhicitta and emptiness are more like two facets of the same diamond. Tibetan Buddhists say that some people achieve Enlightenment by first realizing bodhicitta, and from that, realizing emptiness, whereas others first realize emptiness and through that realization come to realize bodhicitta.

The Buddhist formulation appears to reflect a significant difference from Christianity. Christianity teaches us to love one another as we love ourselves, while the Buddhist would say there is no independently existing self or other to love. However, in different ways both are expressing nonduality.

There is a similarity between what Tibetan Buddhists call real-ization of emptiness and what a Christian might label dying to the old self and being reborn in Christ. Emptiness for Christians is about emptying ourselves of all that prevents us from being open to the presence of God within us and in all things, about abandon-ing (in Thomas Merton's terms) our false self in favor of our true self. Meister Eckhart would say, in terms that sound very close to Buddhist phrasing, that rising in Christ, becoming one with Christ, means to be dead to the self, to cease to regard the individual soul as its own being. We must let go of our egos and become absorbed into the community that is Christ. For Buddhists there is an emptying out of the self but no "filling up" with something else, so to speak, whereas as Christians we become empty so that we may be filled with Christ.

For both Buddhists and Christians there is emptying or moving beyond how we usually view things so that we can see them without our ordinary preconceived human ideas—without delu-sion (Buddhist) and with the eyes of Christ (Christian). Tom Chetwynd opined "that Shakyamuni Buddha and Jesus Christ, in their very Buddhahood and their Christhood most especially, were forerunners of this worldview arising from non-ego—a lim-itless and eternal view that they shared with their followers." Each of them saw, Chetwynd suggests, "what religion had always been leading us toward and pointing at: the essential nature of life, ordinary conscious life—which we each can get to know with clarity and intimacy."[26]

NATURE OF THE MIND

In some respects the way Buddhists talk about the nature of mind and the effect of delusions resembles how Christians talk about the effect of original sin on the soul. Buddhism and Christianity share a belief in the fundamental goodness of the human person, a goodness marred in the one case by delusions and in the other by original sin.

Buddhism views the nature of mind to be clear and luminous. Christians view humans as created in the image of God and created for full union with God, believing God's words in Jeremiah, "Before I formed you in the womb I knew you" (Jer 1:5). Just as for Buddhists the clarity of the mind is muddied by the root delusions of ignorance, attachment, and aversion (all other delusions flow from these three), in Christianity original sin renders humans subject to ignorance and suffering. The goal in each case is to return to a state unmarred by delusion or sin.

There are important differences between the Christian and Buddhist understandings of the nature of the mind. For Buddhists, ridding ourselves of delusions is purely a function of individual effort—we save ourselves. Christians require God's grace to overcome the effect of original sin. So the Buddhist sits alone to rid the mind of delusions; the Christian sits in prayer with God, seeking to gradually unite his will with God's.

Another difference is that for Christians, full union with God is possible only at death; Augustine, for example, believed that we begin contemplation in this life but that it can be perfected only in death. Buddhists, on the other hand, believe it is possible to achieve a fully clear mind in this lifetime. On this point, B. Alan Wallace raises the question whether this is simply because Christian contemplatives never attained the same achievements in contemplation that Buddhists did. In *Mind in the Balance*, he asks: "If Christians had achieved the same levels of meditative stabilization as those claimed by Buddhists, might they have altered their views about the potentials of contemplative practices in this lifetime?"[27] I suspect the difference here is more one of theology than of different levels of achievements in contemplation.

Finally, Christians talk of the purification of the soul, but Buddhists do not believe in a permanently existing soul. Rather, Buddhism views the mind as a series of moments of consciousness, each of which is affected by what came before it. Buddhists do not, of course, use the term "soul," but Buddhist descriptions of the deepest levels of consciousness sound suspiciously like a soul, albeit not unchanging and unitary.

Although Buddhists do not speak of God the way the Judeo-Christian tradition does, there is a striking similarity in the understanding of the true nature of the mind—between what a Christian might call her Christ-nature and what a Buddhist might call Buddha-nature and between what Jesus called the Kingdom of Heaven and what Buddhists call Enlightenment.

LIVING IN THE PRESENT MOMENT

One of Richard Rohr's wonderful books is titled *The Naked Now: Learning to See as the Mystics See.* Rohr's basic thrust is that a mature religiosity requires abandoning our pattern of dualistic thinking, that we must learn to live "in the naked now, the 'sacrament of the present moment.'"[28] He talks about the need to "stand back and calmly observe" all that takes place in our lives, a way of seeing that is characteristic of spiritual sages in all cultures and religions. Wisdom, says Rohr, is the freedom to be present. In the sacrament of the present moment, we experience God, and not words and ideas about God. Brother David Steindl-Rast observes that "at that level of intense awareness, all is love. Seeing is love, breathing is love, being is love—love as a belonging that cannot be questioned or doubted."[29]

Although both Rohr and Steindl-Rast speak from a Christian perspective, what they say is also meaningful in Buddhist terms. One of the Buddha's shortest teachings was that in seeing there should be only what is seen, and in hearing, only what is heard. Those words are an admonition to be fully present in the moment. As one instructor of Buddhist meditation elaborated, "the point is to be fully aware of our experience, without adding interpretation or commentary, without getting lost in it, clinging to it, or pushing it away. This means simply being with what is happening right now."[30]

Christianity and Buddhism both say that it is in the present moment that we touch that which is real, whether we call it Ultimate Reality, God, or something else. Only in the "naked now" can we experience what Abraham Maslow calls "peak experiences," those experiences of existential communion that transcend our ordinary experience.

Part of what keeps us from the present moment is the sense of insecurity and incompleteness that stems from our incorrect perceptions of ourselves and the world. Our failure to grasp impermanence and interconnectedness contributes to our sense of insecurity and incompleteness. We are always on the lookout for what will make us more secure and complete. In Christian terms, we might call it a failure to recognize the truth of St. Augustine's oft-repeated phrase, "Our hearts are restless until they rest in you."

In Buddhist terms, Lama Yeshe explained that because we feel incomplete and insecure, we constantly look outside of ourselves to find someone or something that will make us feel fulfilled and whole. We see an attractive person or object and think, "If only I had such-and-such, *then* I would be happy!" That impulse, he explains, leads us to "turn the object into an idol, overestimating its attractive qualities until it bears little resemblance to its actual nature." Such overestimation is a prescription for disaster, regardless of whether or not we succeed in obtaining the object of our desire. If we are unsuccessful, we are distraught at our inability to possess that which we believe will make us happy. If we succeed, we find ourselves in possession of someone or something that is incapable of providing lasting satisfaction, "something that is as imperfect, incomplete and impermanent as we are ourselves. This person or thing may indeed give us some momentary pleasure, but it can never begin to live up to the expectations we have loaded upon it."[31] Thus we continue to desire more, thinking, "if only he were..." or "if only it was...," constantly looking for something beyond what we have, a way of thinking that makes it impossible for us to stay in the present moment.

We need both to overcome our incorrect notions about ourselves and the world and to change our habits of living in the past and future—learning, as the subtitle of Rohr's book instructs, to see as the mystics see, to live in the naked now. This is something recognized by both Christians and Buddhists.

GRATITUDE

I left gratitude for last, giving it its own place although I might have included it with the shared values of compassion, forgiveness, and generosity. I wanted to separate it from my discussion of those other values having to do with the relationship between and among human beings, in order to emphasize gratitude as a fundamental attitude that affects tremendously who and what we are in the world, regardless of our religious beliefs.

The secular view of the self as an autonomous individual primarily concerned with self-preservation and self-promotion has a corresponding view of the relation of the self to the material things of this world. In simplest terms a society that takes a self-existent, separated view of individuals and that has a culture of individual motivation and achievement tends to promote a culture of entitlement, in which we see the things around us as entitlements, rather than as gifts. My property is "mine" and my achievements are solely the product of "my" effort and talents.

All religious traditions promote a different attitude, one of gratitude. From a Christian standpoint, all we are and all we have are gifts from a loving God. The crucial first step of the Ignatian *examen* is to look back over the day in gratitude, giving thanks for all of the gifts—large and small—that we received over the course of the day. "Whatever you do in word or deed, do all in the name of the Lord Jesus, giving thanks through Him to God the Father," St. Paul told the Colossians (Col 3:17).

The Buddhist belief is that when we develop a sense of gratitude, loving kindness flows naturally; gratitude breaks down the barriers that appear to separate us. A significant thrust of the Tibetan Buddhist meditation on what is termed the "perfect human rebirth" (one of the meditations I adapt for Christians in Part III) is to help us develop a sense of gratitude for all we have been given, spurring us to use our gifts wisely. Gratitude is a vital virtue in other faith traditions as well: Thanksgiving permeates Jewish prayer, entire book chapters are devoted to the development of gratitude in Sufism, and so forth.

The value of a stance of gratitude is easy to see. I believe that if we could effect no change other than to replace an attitude of entitlement with one of gratitude, that change alone would be enough to transform the entire world. When you see everything as your entitlement, your due, it is it hard to do without things, and hard to share the things you have. But seeing everything as a gift for which you are grateful changes everything. Gratefulness helps strengthen our sense of connectedness to God and to each other. It softens the ego and eliminates the barriers between the self and others. Ron Rolheiser speaks of gratitude as the "ultimate virtue." Gratitude, even more so than love, makes us saints "because love is only real when it's fueled by gratitude. If it's fueled by resentment or duty, it's going to cause resentment or be manipulative. If someone asks, 'Who's the most saintly person you know?' I would say the most grateful person."[32]

With regular practice, gratitude becomes a habit of the mind. We wake up each day giving thanks for the blessings of the new day. We spontaneously during the day, almost without thought, find ourselves expressing "Thank you, God." We find ourselves living in a space of blessing and gratitude.

* * *

There is much that is shared between Buddhism and Christianity, indeed, among all of the major world religions. This should not come as a surprise to those who believe in one God. If there is only one God, we can all experience only that one God, whether we label it an experience of God, Ultimate Reality, or something else.

Moreover, whether we acknowledge it or not, different religions have influenced each other over the years. The Jewish Essene sect, which likely influenced John the Baptist and perhaps Jesus, were themselves influenced by Pythagoras and the Greek tradition, which in turn was influenced by the Indian mystical tradition. There were Buddhists living in the Middle East in the centuries following Christ and it is believed that their influence is seen in the way in which monasticism (which was not an element of Judaism or of the Semitic culture) arose in the Christian West. And the social gospel of Christ clearly has exerted influence on both Buddhism and Hinduism.

I don't wish to minimize the differences between Buddhism and Christianity, some of which are quite significant. The Buddhist and Christian understandings of suffering and of the role of suffering are quite divergent. The ways in which Buddhists and Christians talk about desire are very different. The Buddhist understanding that everything we experience is a product of causes and conditions we have created has no room for the Christian understanding of the presence and role of God's grace. The (particularly Tibetan) Buddhist view of the body is in stark contrast to the Christian doctrine of the dignity of the human person created in the image and likeness of God. Nonetheless, the sharing of many underlying dynamics is both undeniable and understandable.

B. Alan Wallace has suggested that the existence of such convergences is important evidence that religion has meaning. If, at the deepest level, religions were truly different, wouldn't that be evidence that individual religions were all just following their own made-up trajectories? The deep convergences tell us something about the validity of those truths.

The convergences also prepare us to consider the value of looking outside of our own faith tradition to enhance our prayer experience. And it is to that I now turn.

PART II

ADAPTING PRAYER PRACTICES FROM ANOTHER FAITH TRADITION

Chapter 3

The Importance of Prayer and Affective Experience

Human beings have a natural inclination toward the transcendent, and prayer is an expression of that inclination. The impulse to pray precedes theology and belief; "wherever one finds humans, one finds humans at prayer."[1] Thus, it is no surprise that prayer and prayerful contemplation or meditation occupy an important place in all faith traditions.

Different people use the terms "prayer," "meditation," and "contemplation" in different ways. Some think of prayer as referring only to communication with God that we initiate—our talking to God or asking something of God—reserving the term "contemplation" for listening to God. Others draw distinctions between meditation and contemplation: Some use the term "meditation" to refer to the process of training the mind and "contemplation" to refer to an action having as its object gaining insight into the nature of reality. Others use the term "meditation" to refer to an analytical or intellectual process and "contemplation" to a process that does not involve discursive thought.

Richard Rohr uses the term "prayer" in a broad sense as "the umbrella word for any interior journeys or practices that allow you to experience faith, hope, and love within yourself."[2] From my Ignatian training, I use "prayer" in a similarly broad fashion, referring to prayer simply as communication between humans and God (or whatever label a person gives to the Ultimate Reality that transcends human existence), a *mutual* communication that includes both our speaking to God and listening to God, and that sometimes uses words and sometimes is wordless. As is apparent from that definition, I use the term broadly enough to include things others might separately label contemplation or meditation. Thus, although I do speak of adapting Tibetan Buddhist analytical meditations for Christians, I otherwise use the terms meditation and prayer interchangeably throughout the book.

As my emphasis on "mutual" suggests, my primary motivation for using the term prayer is to underscore that the activity in which Christians are engaged is a dialogic process with God. This mutuality reflects a fundamental difference between Buddhism and Christianity. Buddhists view meditation as an act you engage in on your own; there is no partner in dialogue. Enlightenment or liberation from the cycle of birth, death, and rebirth in which we exist (termed samsara)—is achieved by individual mental effort. In contrast, Christian prayer always involves more than the self. Christians recognize their need for God and their dependence on God's grace; the first of the Beatitudes, "blessed are the poor in spirit" (Mt 5:3), acknowledges that ultimate dependence. Christian mystics, Hugo Enomiya-Lassalle observes, "do not speak of enlightenment, even in other words, as something independent of grace. They always presuppose grace."[3] Using the term prayer rather than meditation—regardless of the form that prayer takes—serves as a reminder that, as Christians, we are engaged in an activity in which God is involved, rather than a solitary endeavor.

Why is prayer so important? Why is prayer essential if we are to grow spiritually?

In St. Matthew's Gospel, Jesus tells the chief priests and elders the story of two sons (Mt 21:28–32). The father asks each of them to go out and work in the vineyard. The first tells his father he will not, but eventually does the work his father asked of him. The second assures the father he will do as he asks, but never does so.

In a sermon I once heard on that passage, the priest spoke of "rhetorical Christians." Rhetorical Christians, he said, are great at telling you what they believe. They believe Jesus Christ is their Lord and Master and that there is no salvation other than through him. They believe all the right things and they say all the right things. They are willing to shout all of these beliefs from the roof-tops. They talk a good game about what they believe, but their lives bear no evidence of their beliefs.

As the saying goes, however, talk is cheap. Too cheap to justify the use of the term Christian, as illustrated by the story of the two sons: When Jesus asks his audience which of the two actually did the will of the father, they have no difficulty correctly identifying the first.

Being a Christian, a follower of Christ, is not about giving intellectual assent to a checklist of beliefs. Rather, what Christ seeks from those who would call themselves his disciples is a fundamental transformation of heart and mind—a transformation that changes everything about who we are in the world. Jesus' teaching of the Beatitudes (Mt 5:3–12) can lead to no other conclusion; poverty of spirit, purity of heart, meekness, and the rest, are qualities we are asked to embrace in our hearts, not merely ideas to which we give intellectual assent.

Because what Christianity seeks is a total transformation of mind and heart, prayer is an essential component of the Christian path, particularly affective experiences in prayer, experiences that touch our hearts. The theologian Karl Rahner puts great stress on the personal and experiential aspects of God's communication of Godself with us. A foundational element of Rahner's thought is that God is accessible to ordinary human experience and that we need experiential knowledge of God, not merely conceptual knowledge.

Thus, despite the fact that we are intellectual beings and we love to use our minds, we need to recognize that transformation is not ultimately an experience of the intellect (although the intellect plays a role in the conversion process). Rather, conversion is an experience of the heart. For, as Jesus explains to his disciples, "out of the heart come evil thoughts, murders, adulteries, fornications, thefts, false witness, slanders. These are the things which defile the man" (Mt 15:19–20).

By way of illustration, there are some fundamental Christian truths, perhaps the most basic of which has to do with the extent of God's love for us. A key to spiritual growth is embracing God's unconditional love and fidelity.

It is very easy to mouth the words, "Of course I know that God loves me unconditionally. I know I can never lose that love." The words are easy to speak, but what we seek, what we need, what will affect who we are in the world, is knowledge and understanding at the level of the heart—knowing to the core of our being—that God loves us unconditionally. That there is nothing we can do to make God love us any less. Such deep knowledge can only be gained through actual religious experience. The writings of Teresa of Avila illustrate this well. It is clear that Teresa's contemplative prayer opened her to the reality of God's love, a realization that led her to center her life completely on God. You will find the same in the writings of Christian mystics as diverse as Julian of Norwich and Thomas Merton.

Connected with this deep realization of God's love is realizing at a deep level that we cannot be separated from the God who loves us endlessly and unconditionally. It is only with that knowledge that we can actualize the central Christian command to love one another, a command that includes loving our enemies. Loving others—including our enemies—is not something that can be forced as a matter of will. It requires a fundamental change in our inner being, a change that stems from gaining a deep realization of ourselves as the beloved of God and our nature as interrelated with God and others. Loving expansively as God does—a love that takes in those who are not good to us—is impossible so long as we see a division between others and ourselves.

If we could see God in ourselves and in others, if we could see how intimately related we are to God, if we could see interconnectedness of all life with each other and with God, it would change everything. One of Thomas Merton's foundational religious experiences was just such a realization. In *Conjectures of a Guilty Bystander*, he describes being "suddenly overwhelmed with the realization that I loved all those people, that they were mine and I theirs, that we could not be alien to one another even though we were total strangers." He described himself as feeling as if he had awoken "from a dream of separateness, or spurious self-isolation in a special world, the world of renunciation and supposed holiness." This had an extraordinary effect on Merton. He describes his realization in words that make clear he is not conveying something that he worked out intellectually:

> It was as if I suddenly saw the secret beauty of their hearts, the depths of their hearts where neither sin nor desire nor self-knowledge can reach, the core of their reality, the person that each one is in God's eyes. If only they could all see themselves as they really *are*. If only we could see each other that way all the time. There would be no more war, no more hatred, no more cruelty, no more greed....I suppose the big problem would be that we would fall down and worship each other. But this cannot be *seen*, only believed and "understood" by a peculiar gift.[4]

The aim of Christian contemplative prayer, then, is this kind of affective experience described by Merton—an experience that touches our heart as well as our head so that we are able to integrate important truths about God and our relationship to God and others at a much deeper level than we could if we were just thinking about them.

If you have read any of the experiences of the Christian mystics, you already have some understanding of what I have been saying. Ursula King defines a mystic in this way: "A mystic is a person who is deeply aware of the powerful presence of the divine spirit: someone who seeks, above all, the knowledge and love of God and who experiences to an extraordinary degree the profoundly personal encounter with the energy of divine life."[5] Robert Ellwood says that mysticism is *the* cardinal means toward ultimate transformation. He describes mystical experience as an "experience in a religious context that is immediately or subsequently interpreted by the experiencer as an encounter with ultimate divine reality in a direct nonrational way that engenders a deep sense of unity and of living during the experience on a level of being other than the ordinary."[6]

Roger Corless speaks of the power of the mystical experience to reform our lives. Direct contact with God "inspires us to do all sorts of heroic and good things by the very attractiveness of his presence. Laws, in such a condition are unnecessary, for the mystic observes them, 'naturally, as if by habit,' as St. Benedict says. 'Love God and do what you like,' said Augustine."[7]

What is true of Christianity is no less true of Buddhism, which also emphasizes experiential knowledge gained in meditation. From a Buddhist perspective, suffering comes from an untamed mind, the mind suffering under delusions of attachment, aversion, and ignorance. Meditation helps us to both recognize that we are under the sway of delusions and develop the wisdom necessary to remedy these root causes of suffering. Tibetan lamas consistently emphasize that we cannot gain that wisdom merely by hearing someone talk about concepts. Even if we listen to the words of someone who has perfectly realized a truth, we cannot gain a full understanding and deep appreciation of that truth from her description. Kensur Losang Thubten Rinpoche illustrated with the simple example of taste: Someone who has actually tasted sugarcane knows how it is sweet—he can taste its sweetness. What happens when another person comes along, someone who has never tasted sugarcane, and asks, "What does the sugarcane taste like?" How, he asked, can anyone express a meaningful answer to that question simply by saying it is sweet? Only through the direct experience of that person tasting the sugarcane could the person apprehend exactly what is the sweetness of the sugarcane.[8]

Similarly, Lama Thubten Zopa Rinpoche and Lama Yeshe wrote that because Buddhist teachings can be presented in a logical manner, "it is easy to feel that the knowledge to be gained from them is merely intellectual. You become fascinated by the intricacy and thoroughness of Buddhist philosophy and its technical vocabulary, and eagerly grasp at the words of particular Dharma explanations. Such intellectualization without actualization is only a source of mental conflict."[9]

Words are insufficient. Collecting intelligence is insufficient. Only by engaging in meditation can we have the experience necessary to achieve a fully awakened mind.

Although I have less familiarity with Zen Buddhism than with Tibetan or Theravadan Buddhism, my reading suggests that this emphasis is even greater in Zen. The focus of Zen is practice—actual meditation experience—with very little, if any, discussion of theological concepts.

Again by way of illustration, just as in Christianity, there are some fundamental Buddhist truths. One of those, as I discussed in chapter 2, is impermanence, the idea that everything in the physical world is impermanent, changing all the time. Everything constantly rises and vanishes. Some of those changes are easily apprehended, but others are more subtle. But whether visible or subtle, everything and everyone changes moment by moment. Everything is impermanent and in flow, arising and passing away moment to moment. Consciousness, the object of which we are conscious, all the different mental factors, the body—all phenomena share this impermanence.

Now, I can say, "Everything is impermanent," and any Buddhist will nod his or her head in agreement and say yes, that is true. But it is one thing to say—and even think—that everything is impermanent; it is another to realize it at a level where it can make a difference. It is possible to intellectually understand impermanence without really fully apprehending it. As a result, despite what we may understand intellectually, instinctively we cling to people and things as if they were permanent and unchanging. (In fact, we don't want the nice person or the beautiful object to change.) And we cling especially strongly to our view of our own person.

The divergence between our intellectual understanding of the concept of impermanence and the habitual way our minds work is particularly strong in the case of things we desire and label as attractive. At the intellectual level, we are aware that our beautiful girlfriend or boyfriend will not always be beautiful and that our treasured new sports car will not last forever. But that intellectual awareness is not matched by a deep realization. Lama Yeshe explains that

> if we check our deep, heartfelt attitude towards what we
> desire, we will discover a habitual grasping for permanence
> that remains basically untouched by whatever intellectual

understanding of the process of change we may have. Just look at the way our heart shakes with anticipation when we are caught up in strong desire for someone or something. Would we experience such intense agitation if we did not hold the unrealistic expectations that we do?[10]

The only way to gain a deep realization of impermanence is through an actual experience in meditation, a Buddhist belief confirmed by my own experience with vipassana meditation, sometimes called insight meditation, which I address more extensively in chapter 20. Vipassana is a meditation practice that combines concentration and mindfulness. The practice requires keeping your awareness on the experience of the present moment—starting with the rising and falling of the abdomen as you inhale and exhale, and then moving on to an awareness of your posture, and ultimately to a moment-by-moment awareness of your sense experiences and feelings. The idea is to simply be aware, letting each object of consciousness simply rise and vanish. To not hold onto the past or worry about the future, but simply relax into what is happening in the present moment, without judgment or evaluation.

In Thailand I did an almost four-month vipassana meditation retreat—fifteen weeks of alternating periods of sitting and walking meditation from the time I woke up until the time I went to sleep, broken only by a daily meeting with my instructor, eating, and attending to other physical needs. I broke that routine only once, after almost three months, to take a quick trip to Malaysia to renew my visa. During that retreat I had a very strong experience of impermanence, of actually experiencing everything (including myself) as changing moment by moment. The example I always use to describe the experience is the sensation you have standing at the edge of the beach as the waves roll in and the sand recedes from under your feet—that there is nothing solid you can hold onto.

The affective experience of vipassana meditation allows the meditator to develop insight by actually experiencing impermanence. We actually see...feel...experience things rising and vanishing. Buddhists explain that the depth of that experience is what leads us to an understanding that whatever we experience in this life—whether pleasant or unpleasant—is inherently incapable of providing more than temporary happiness. In Buddhist terms, we gain a deep realization of the inherent unsatisfactoriness of the cycle of birth and rebirth that we suffer.

Although I don't have sufficient knowledge to make the claim that this emphasis on affective prayer experience is expressed equally strongly in all religions, it is clear that Buddhism and Christianity are not alone in this regard. A similar emphasis on direct, experiential knowledge is found in Hinduism, for example, where yoga practice is designed to unite the human spirit with God.

This shared understanding of the importance of affective experience in prayer may help explain the widespread use of poetry in so many prayer traditions. In poetry, language is used for its evocative qualities in addition to the literal meaning of the words used, and poetry seeks an emotional or sensual response rather than an intellectual one. Poetry, because it operates at the level of our affect and not our intellect, can help us attain that heartfelt, affective knowledge I have been talking about. Hafiz writes, "A poet is someone who can pour light in a cup, then raise it to nourish your beautiful parched holy mouth." Rumi saw as the primary purpose of his poetry, not to explain Sufism, but to stir up love and to help people "realize that as human beings, they are bound by their very nature to turn to God and to devote themselves totally to Him."[11]

The shared understanding of the importance of affective experience also helps explain why many religious traditions make use of symbolic and ritualistic bodily actions, which move the worshipper beyond the intellect into the heart. Hindus engage in ritual washing before kneeling on their prayer shawls. Buddhists do prostrations. Jews touch their prayer shawls to the Torah as it is processed during certain ceremonies. Catholics genuflect when entering a church and carry up to the altar in offering the bread and wine that will be consecrated in the Eucharist. In each of these cases the union of the physical act with the mind creates a powerful effect. One of the lamas used to tell his students that if they were doing prostrations without the visualizations and prayers intended to accompany them they might as well just go to the gym rather than engage in empty ritual. The Congregation for the Doctrine of the Faith sounded a similar caution in its 1989 *Letter to American Bishops on Some Aspects of Christian Meditation*, warning that "psychophysical symbolism" could easily become an obstacle to true prayer if we fail to remember that the body is symbolic and that bodily sensations themselves are not necessarily indications of spiritual experiences.[12]

Finally, the shared understanding of the importance of affective experience may also help explain the emphasis on oral transmission in Christianity, Buddhism, and other faiths. Christians listen to the proclamation of the Word of God at worship services. Buddhists receive oral transmissions of important texts from lamas. When we hear the Word proclaimed, something happens that is different from when we read words on a page. When I close my eyes and listen to the reading of the Gospel at Mass I feel and experience the events that are described in a way that touches a place deeper than the intellect.

Prayer forms may differ across faith traditions and there may be a different way of articulating the aim of prayer. There may even be different conceptions of to whom one is praying. Some say God; others have a less defined sense of the object of their prayer, but that may matter a whole lot less than it appears on the surface. One religious practitioner who self-identifies as Jewish-Buddhist, wrote, "I generally do not think about a 'to whom' when I pray. Prayer, when it is happening, is what my heart feels like doing. And when I do feel that my prayers are directed, it is the connection that feels good to me, and I don't think about 'to whom.'"[13] I recall a conversation I had with my daughter when she was quite young. At a time when I was still a Buddhist, we were talking about prayer. She explained to me that some nights she prayed to God, some nights to Buddha, and some nights to Uncle Blaise (a beloved uncle of mine who had recently died). It all seemed to work for her. Although as Christians we are very conscious of to whom we are praying—be it God the Father, Jesus, or the Holy Spirit, what is most important is union with the divine.

One of the things I learned from having spent time both as a Buddhist and as a Christian, however, is that the closer one gets to talking or hearing about actual religious experience the less difference one finds between expressions of those religious experiences by pray-ers of different faith traditions. I recall the first time I read the writings of Teresa of Avila after my return to Catholicism from Buddhism. My reaction was that I could change six or seven words in her descriptions of her religious experience and place them in a Buddhist text and no one would suspect they had been written by a Christian. The Dalai Lama once expressed a similar thought about a prayer attributed to St. Francis: when he heard it, he thought he was listening to someone read from a Buddhist text. In a similar vein, D. T. Suzuki has explored the congruence between the experiences of the medieval Christian mystic Meister Eckhart and those of Zen Buddhism. If you spend any amount of time reading descriptions of people's religious experiences, you will discover the same thing. The religious experiences of Jews, of Buddhists, of Christians (and doubtless others) have similar characteristics.

There is a certain intuitive sense to this. All religion has its origin in experiences of the sacred. There is only one truth; there is only one ultimate reality. Deepak Chopra writes, "Consciousness is universal, and if there is such a thing as God-consciousness, no one can be excluded from it."[14] How we encounter that ultimate reality may be different and our individual experiences won't be identical, but we can recognize, hear, the truth of the other's experience. Even scholars like Stephen Prothero, who argue vehemently against minimizing the differences among religions, admit that those differences are less significant for mystics than for those without such religious experiences.

To be sure, how people understand and translate their mystical experiences will be colored by their a priori religious beliefs. Henri De Lubac says that mystical experiences are inextricable from the belief systems of those who have them. He argues that those who focus on similarities between the mystical experiences of people of different religions pay insufficient attention to the differences among the faith traditions in which the experiences occur. I think it is more accurate to say that it is not the experiences that are different, but how we talk about them and understand their significance. If you listen carefully to the different words a Christian and a Buddhist use to describe their prayer experience, you will—as my experience with Teresa of Avila suggests—hear the common chords.

Ultimately, whether or not you accept that the experiences of mystics of different faith traditions resemble each other is of little consequence to your ability to benefit from the meditations in Part III. In many of the meditations, you will see that the aim sought by a particular Buddhist meditation is similar, or identical, to a Christian aim. In other cases, even if the Buddhist might express the aim in different terms, as the next chapter explains, there is still good reason to think that a Christian can benefit from prayer experiences adapted from the Tibetan tradition.

Chapter 4

Why Look to Tibetan Buddhism?

The importance of affective prayer and mystical experiences across faith traditions does not itself answer the question of why we might look outside of our own faith tradition to find ways to pray. Why should Christians think there is anything in Tibetan Buddhism that might enrich our prayer life?

As then Cardinal Ratzinger recognized, in a 1989 letter to Catholic bishops issued by the Congregation of the Doctrine of the Faith, "genuine practices of non-Christian meditation" may "constitute a suitable means of helping the person who prays to come before God."[1] Similarly, the letter *Dominus Iesus*, issued in 2000, acknowledges that prayers and rituals from other faith religious traditions may be "occasions or pedagogical helps in which the human heart is prompted to be open to the action of God."[2]

The idea of Christians learning from Buddhism and Buddhist meditation is not a new one. Indeed, as Raimon Panikkar once observed, "the whole history of Christianity is one of enrichment and renewal brought about by elements that came from outside itself."[3] The Centering Prayer that has been popularized by Trappist monk Thomas Keating and others is as inspired by Eastern meditation as it is by the experience of the early Desert Fathers. The same is true of the Christian contemplative meditation taught by Benedictine monk John Main. Christian Zen meditation is becoming increasingly popular and has long been often offered at Catholic retreat houses in the United States. As early as the mid-1960s, the Jesuit Hugo Enomiya Lassale recognized that "practiced the right way, Zen could be useful to anyone regardless of his religious conviction and denomination."[4] Thus, my suggestion that Christians can benefit from Tibetan Buddhist analytical meditations mines a new branch of a vein that has already been opened by others.

There are two basic categories of Tibetan Buddhist meditation: stabilization, or concentrative, meditation and analytical meditation. The aim of the former is to combat the mind's usual practice of jumping from one object of attention to another. Concentration is necessary for any form of meditation, and so stabilization techniques seek to calm the mind and help us develop the ability to focus single-pointedly on an object until the mind can rest effortlessly on that object for significant periods of time. There are various stabilization methods, many of which use the breath as an object of concentration.

The second category is analytical meditation, which makes use of our faculties of intellect and imagination. The goal is to come to a clear and unshakable conclusion as to the truth of Buddhist teachings and how things truly exist. This is achieved by an active process of investigating the object of attention of the meditation session. The imagination often comes into play, as the meditator visualizes certain scenarios and situations as a means of investigation. Powers of logical reasoning are also brought into play as a means of exploring the relevant aspects of the subject of meditation in order to develop a clear understanding of the subject.

Kathleen McDonald, an American who has been a Tibetan Buddhist nun since 1974, explains that in one sense analytical meditation is akin to studying a subject, but it is a study engaged in at a deep level of concentration and involving a certain subtlety of thought. McDonald explains that "the first step in gaining any real insight is to understand *conceptually* how things are. This conceptual clarity develops into firm conviction, which, when combined with stabilizing meditation, brings direct and intuitive knowing."[5] As McDonald suggests, analytical and stabilization meditations are often used in combination. I might begin a meditation session using stabilization meditation to develop a level of concentration. In that concentrated state, I would then engage in an analytical meditation. Then, when some understanding—some insight or firm conclusion about how things exist—is gained, I would then keep the focus on that understanding, allowing it to really sink in. The final stage is crucial. We must both analyze the subject and then place concentrated attention on the result of the analysis.

This description of a Buddhist meditative process combining analytical and stabilization meditation is quite similar to descriptions of the Christian practice of *Lectio Divina*. In that prayer practice, after pondering a word or phrase of scripture, savoring the reading, listening, and then dialoguing with God about the ideas the reflection on the scripture has generated, the invitation is to rest in silence, letting go of words. When we have an apprehension of truth, the idea is to simply sit in that apprehension without engaging in further thought.

There are also some striking similarities between Tibetan analytical meditations and Ignatian contemplation, a Catholic prayer form that aims at experiencing the kind of affective, or heartfelt, knowledge I described in chapter 3, and which has been a regular part of my prayer practice for a number of years. They employ a similar method, each making extensive use of the imagination to help us to gain understanding of deep truths. Both also aim at generating knowledge that goes beyond concepts—that is, at a deep intuitive (Buddhist) or affective (Ignatian) level.

Ignatian contemplation is a way of praying with scripture that involves putting ourselves in a Gospel scene as a participant in that scene. We enter into an actual episode from the life of Jesus as a participant, which allows us to interact with Jesus and the people with whom he came into contact. Doing this allows us to experience God in a direct and personal manner.

To better understand Ignatian contemplation, think of what happens to you when you are deeply engrossed in a novel or in a friend's description of a recent vacation. As you read or listen, it is as though you were there. Your mind conjures up images of the experience and you can almost smell and taste what is being described. When we listen to someone tell a story or when we read a novel, we let ourselves be placed into the event—we are there. We do the same thing when we recall a singular event in our life. We forget we are sitting in a room listening or reading or thinking—instead we become part of the event or episode being described.

Ignatian contemplation uses this activity we do all of the time, but with a piece of scripture as the inspiration. We read the passage we are praying with, set the scene, enter the scene, and allow it to unfold. We watch, we listen, we notice, and we interact with the characters there. We speak, we are spoken to. We respond to what we see and hear. We put ourselves in the scene as a participant—we let Jesus wash our feet, we stand with Jesus in the Jordan watching him be baptized by John, we listen to Jesus telling us he will be put to death, we help Andrew pass around the multiplied loaves to the thousands. We feel the stillness of the paralytic as Jesus reaches out to touch him. We feel the grief of Mary when Jesus leaves Nazareth. So we are not merely spectators, we really enter into the action. And just as a Tibetan Buddhist analytical meditation moves from analysis to placing concentrated attention on the insight gained from the analysis, in Ignatian contemplation we stay with strong feelings or insights that arise during the imaginative prayer.

The result of this kind of prayer is beyond comprehension. The prayer itself is an experience, as real and as memorable as any other real event. Although we pick the passage and use our imagination to set up the scene and enter into it, how the scene unfolds, where it takes us and what happens during the prayer is determined by God. We cannot predict what will happen. God works in God's ways, so sometimes what God wants to convey relates to what you thought you were asking, and other times God may decide you need to hear a different message.

That last observation highlights a fundamental difference between Ignatian contemplation and Buddhist analytical meditations. Buddhist analytical meditations are viewed as solely a process of the consciousness of the individual engaged in the meditation. Ignatian contemplation, in contrast, is a dialogic process with God. Thus, for example, where conversation with Jesus is not a natural part of the scripture scene as it unfolds, the recommendation is to end the session with a colloquy, St. Ignatius's term for talking with Jesus about what has transpired during the prayer.

There are other differences as well. Ignatian contemplation is a method of praying with scripture, so some biblical passage will generally be the prompt for the meditation, whereas Buddhist analytical mediations do not proceed from a purely scriptural base. Finally, Ignatian contemplation does not necessarily (although it may, depending on how the scene unfolds) involve the type of analysis and reasoning employed in Tibetan Buddhist analytical meditations.

Notwithstanding these differences, the similarity of approach gives good reason to think something might be found for Christians in the process of Tibetan analytical meditations. More important, the content of many of the analytical meditations provides even more reason to think they might be valuable for Christians.

The essential points of the teaching of the Buddha were condensed into a text composed by the eleventh-century Buddhist teacher Atisha titled *The Lamp Illustrating the Path* (sometimes translated as *The Light of the Lamp of the Path to Enlightenment*). Subsequently, the Tibetan Buddhist master Je Tzongkhapa expanded on Atisha's teachings in the *Lam-Rim Chenmo* (*The Great Exposition on the Gradual Path to Enlightenment*). The word "lam" means path and "rim" means a systematic, sequential order. As its title suggests, the *Lam-Rim* presents a series of teachings and meditations designed to transform the mind. It is a step-by-step method of practice, a gradual path for the transformation of the mind by ridding it of delusions.

The *Lam-Rim* contains three different levels of teaching, meant for practitioners with different levels of capacity. The levels are distinguished from one another in terms of motivation. The lowest level is concerned with the desire to avoid an unfortunate rebirth in the next life. The teachings and meditations in this level focus on understanding impermanence, the reality of death, and the need to live a moral life. The intermediate level seeks liberation from the cycle of birth and rebirth. It seeks to bring about the cessation of suffering by eliminating the cause of suffering. The highest level aims at achieving enlightenment for the sake of all sentient beings, a term that includes all beings who suffer the cycle of birth and rebirth, whether humans or animals, on earth or in hell or heavenly realms. This highest level involves the wish to become a bodhisattva—a being who seeks enlightenment with the motivation of freeing others from their suffering.

Many of the meditations intended for those of higher capacity and motivation are aimed at combating the self-cherishing mind and cultivating bodhicitta—the mind that renounces the self and cherishes others. From a Tibetan Buddhist standpoint, the self-cherishing attitude is the source of obstacles for practicing

Dharma. It is believed that unless we abandon self-cherishing thoughts, it is impossible to develop the mind. In cultivating bodhicitta, the mind that cherishes others over ourselves, we develop the motivation to help all beings without distinction, the ability to cherish all others over the self—regardless of how they behave toward us. Equanimity is sometimes framed as one of the aims, to remind us that universal compassion extends to all, allowing us to love our enemies as well as our friends.

It is easy to see the potential of the highest level of teachings—those aimed at combating the self-cherishing mind and seeking the good of others—to be of benefit to Christians. Indeed, it is likely that the life and teachings of Christ had an impact on the development of the Mahayana Buddhist ideal of becoming a bodhisattva. Like other aspects of Mahayana Buddhism, the bodhisattva ideal had it origin outside of India, where Buddhism originally arose.

Other of the *Lam-Rim* meditations aim to promote an understanding of emptiness, which is not unrelated to gaining both an appreciation for what Christians might refer to as the distinction between the true self and the false self, and an understanding of what it means to die to self and rise in Christ. These meditations seek to dispel the delusion of independent existence, helping us to see that all things exist in dependence on causes and conditions.

It is possible to talk endlessly about Buddhist versus Christian meditation. But the best way to see how the former might be useful to an adherent of the latter is to turn to the meditations themselves.

PART III

ANALYTICAL MEDITATIONS
AND COMMENTARY

INTRODUCTION

This part presents fifteen Tibetan Buddhist analytic meditations as I have adapted them for Christian prayer, each of which is accompanied by a commentary. Many of the meditations are rooted in the *Lam-Rim Chen Mo*, Je Tsongkhapa's *Graduated Path to Enlightenment*. The *Lam-Rim* is a basic text in the Gelugpa lineage or school of Tibetan Buddhism, which was founded by Lama Tsongkhapa.

Others of the meditations are derived from other texts on thought transformation within Tibetan Buddhism. It is said that all of the Tibetan teachings on thought transformation are condensed in a text by the Kadampa geshe Langri Tangpa, the *Eight Verses of Thought Transformation*, a text that addresses both the development of loving kindness (bodhicitta) and wisdom (emptiness).

The Buddhist tradition places great emphasis on the oral transmission of teachings. I received oral instruction on the *Lam-Rim*, the *Eight Verses*, and other thought transformation texts from Lama Thubten Zopa Rinpoche, who was my root teacher during my years as a Tibetan Buddhist, and from other lamas, including His Holiness the Dalai Lama. I also learned many of the analytical meditations I adapt in this book through guided meditations led either by a lama or by more senior students. Some of what I present here is drawn from my notes of those oral instructions and guided meditations. Other parts are drawn from written commentaries on the central Tibetan texts.

I present here only meditations I have had personal experience with. I have read many things about Buddhism and Buddhist meditation practices that appeared to have been written by people with little or no experience, who write based on what they have read or heard about Buddhism. I am comfortable presenting and recommending to others only what I believe to be beneficial based on my own experience.

In each chapter, I present first my adapted meditation and then the commentary on it. I strongly recommend doing a meditation at least once before reading its accompanying commentary. In this way you can do the meditation without any preconceived idea of what you are "supposed to" experience. The danger of reading too much about a meditation practice before we engage in it is that we then approach the actual meditation with expectations that color our experience. Instead of focusing full attention on doing the meditation, part of the mind is focused on whether our experience matches the understanding we gained from our reading. When I did my first vipassana retreat in Thailand, I received only the most basic instruction in how to do the practice. Only later did I gain a more theoretical understanding of the meditation and its goals. This served me well.

The commentary that follows each meditation explains the Buddhist goals for and principles underlying the meditation, and the reasoning behind the adaptations I made. The commentaries frequently offer relevant Christian biblical references and discuss related Christian doctrines or beliefs that the meditation calls into play. Much of what you will find in the commentary picks up on themes introduced in the first four chapters of the book (especially chapter 2), although it is not necessary to read those chapters first. The commentaries also address problems that sometimes arise in connection with a particular exercise. They do not address general hindrances that arise in meditation, such as distractions, laxity, and excitement; there are many books on meditation that address such general hindrances. You will find a very good discussion of the problems that arise, particularly in the early stages of a meditation practice, in Kathleen McDonald's *How to Meditate: A Practical Guide.*

The first time you practice any of these meditations you may feel some awkwardness. Some of them have very lengthy instructions, meaning that even if you read them through carefully before you start (which I strongly recommend that you do), you may feel as if you are constantly interrupting your meditation to check and see what you should do next. However, after doing a meditation several times, it will no longer feel so disjointed. One way to avoid the initial awkwardness is to do the meditation as a guided meditation, with one person reading the instructions out loud, pausing between segments. This works well with a group but can also be done with a friend. I was first exposed to many of the original Tibetan versions of these meditations precisely in that way.

My expectation is that many of these meditations will come quite easily to you once you become familiar with the instructions. The Buddhist principles involved are sufficiently similar to Christian ideas you are accustomed to that you will not feel any stretch in praying with them. Others will be more challenging. Here I offer the same suggestion I make every time I introduce a new form of prayer to a person or a group—even when it is a prayer that comes out of the person's own tradition: Try it. Try it with as open a mind as you can. If you find it to be helpful, use it. If not, discard it.

This, I believe, is the appropriate approach for everything to do with the spiritual path. Ultimately, the question is what does your experience tell you? You should not evaluate any meditation or practice simply based on what someone tells you, but test it by your own experience and then form a judgment. One of the great contributions of the historical figure we call the Buddha was his emphasis on believing nothing simply because some others say it is true, whether the source is expressed as tradition, authority, hearsay, or something else. Always, we should seek to achieve "direct knowledge." This is true of what the Buddha taught—the Four Noble Truths were the fruit of his meditation experience. It is also true, for example, of the Spiritual Exercises of St. Ignatius, a program of prayers and meditations aimed at developing a deeper conversion to Christian discipleship. What St. Ignatius instructed others to do was based on his own experience, not on anything he read or was told. Both the Buddha and St. Ignatius invite us to have these experiences for ourselves.

We tend to ignore something suggested by what I've just said— that there is a learning process involved in prayer. Tom Chetwynd, an English Christian who is a practitioner of Zen meditation, likened Zen sitting to learning a sport or learning to read. While some forms of prayer come very easily to us, others require practice and it takes us a while to become familiar and comfortable with them.

Let me make some specific suggestions before you move on to the meditations. First, I encourage you to spend at least a few minutes engaging in some exercise to settle your mind before beginning. One possibility is to start with one of the Buddhist or Christian breathing meditations I discuss in chapter 20. I recognize many who struggle to find enough time for their prayer may cringe at the suggestion to engage in a preliminary practice before tackling the meditations here. But just as with the value of stretching before engaging in physical exercise, the analytical meditations will be much more effective if you develop some level of concentration before you begin to pray with them.

Second, be very attentive to your reactions to the meditations, both positive and negative. Where you encounter resistance, spend some time contemplating what it is about the meditation that makes it a challenge or a problem for you. Reflecting on that question itself may reveal some useful things for you. At the same time, note those things that distract you from the meditation. Sometimes distractions are just that—distractions—and can be ignored. ("What should I cook for dinner tonight?") But other times, something that arises during your meditation, particularly if the same "distraction" arises repeatedly, can be a signal that there is something that needs your attention, that requires some work between you and God.

Third, I talked in chapter 4 about the two basic types of Tibetan meditation—stabilization (or concentrative) meditation and analytical meditation—and the fact that they are intended to be used in combination. After you settle your mind into a concentrated state, begin the analytical meditation. Any time you experience a deep insight, a deep sense of realization, stop the analysis and keep your attention focused on that realization. Let it sink in deeply. Only move on to the next point of analysis and reasoning when you feel your attention wavering. Kathleen McDonald explains that "this union of analytical and stabilizing meditations is essential if we are to achieve true mind-transformation. In analytical meditation we think about and understand intellectually a particular point, and through stabilization meditation we gradually make it a part of our very experience of life."[1]

The Dalai Lama illustrated the use of this process in the context of a Christian meditating on love and compassion:

In an analytical aspect of that meditation, we would be thinking along specific lines, such as the following: to truly love God one must demonstrate that love through the action of loving fellow human beings in a genuine way, loving one's neighbor....

These reflections will enable you to develop a deep conviction in the importance and value of compassion and tolerance. Once you arrive at that certain point where you feel totally convinced of the preciousness of and need for compassion and tolerance, you will experience a sense of being touched, a sense of being transformed from within. At this point, you should place your mind single-pointedly in that conviction, without applying any further analysis. Your mind should rather remain single-pointedly in equipoise: this is the absorptive or placement aspect of meditation on compassion. Thus, both types of meditation are applied in one meditation session.[2]

That is the way you should proceed with all of the meditations presented here.

Fourth, many of these meditations ask you to engage in visualization, for example, to visualize Jesus in the space before you or to visualize other human beings. Many Christians, particularly those who engage in Ignatian Contemplation, which I described in chapter 4, and similar prayer forms, are familiar with this process. For those who are not, it is helpful to know that the powers of imagination differ from person to person. Some people have a visual imagination that allows them to "see" in their mind incredibly detailed and vivid scenes, almost as though they were watching a Technicolor movie. Others (like me) tend to see fragments of images, but not entire images or scenes. Other people are able to "hear" or sense things more than "see" them. I put "see" and "hear" in quotes to underscore that we are talking about a faculty of the mind here, not one of the eyes or ears. Some people feel rather than see or hear. Robert Corless uses the term "Emotive Vision." He gives the example of thinking of a good friend whom you have known for a long time, and asks what comes to mind when you think of that person. "Probably nothing very visual. You do not see them in the room but you *feel* as *if* they were in the room. That is an Emotive Vision."[3]

When you engage in these visualizations, you are allowing an image or sound to appear in your mind; it does not actually appear externally to your eyes or ears. The important point is to understand that there is no right or wrong here. Visualize as best as you can, without straining to try to accomplish anything more; the straining will just create tension. Be relaxed and accepting of whatever you experience. Whether your sense is more visual or auditory or impressionistic, the meditation will work for you.

Fifth, several of the meditations include lines of poems or prayers that will be part of your contemplation. The instructions will ask you to slowly pray the lines. Those of us who are used to praying with scripture or other written material will find nothing strange about those instructions. Others may find it disruptive to be asked to read something during their meditation. If that is the case for you, you can always simply pray the words that come to your heart rather than using the provided text.

Three closing comments are in order before moving on to the meditations themselves. First, I want to be very clear at the outset that I am not suggesting this way of praying is better than other ways of praying. I offer these meditations as means of enhancing your existing prayer. There are many types of prayer and most of us will incorporate a number of different prayer forms into our practice. At different times one or another of those forms may be more suitable for us than others. So the question is not: why should I be doing this instead of some other kind of prayer? The question is whether you might want to consider incorporating one or more of these meditations into your current prayer practice, whatever form that current practice takes. That is something you cannot judge without trying them.

Second, as both a spiritual director and someone who has been seeing a spiritual director for at least a decade, I share the view common to the Christian and Buddhist tradition that having a spiritual director or spiritual guide is important for anyone who is a regular and serious pray-er. Intensive prayer brings up many things—some pleasant and some very difficult to deal with. A guide can be very helpful in dealing with the things that surface. It is also the case that our individual discernment can be faulty. Talking about our prayer with a trained spiritual director can help ensure that we do not fall under the sway of delusions. Whenever anyone asks me who would benefit from having a spiritual director, my response is always: anyone with a regular prayer practice who is sincerely interested in deepening his or her religious experience. Many churches maintain lists of spiritual directors in their area and Spiritual Directors International has a "Seek and Find Guide" on its website that can help you find a spiritual director almost anywhere in the world.

Finally, as with anything else, progress on the spiritual journey requires commitment, and a regular prayer practice is an important part of that. Many of us are already daily pray-ers. To those who are not I would encourage you to start. I can promise you that once you get into the habit of daily prayer, it will become as normal a part of your life as your daily shower. Some days you will have less time to pray than on other days. Although many of these meditations are long, you will find that they can often be broken down into shorter segments and, in some instances, I have made specific suggestions for how you might do that. This is your prayer—once you become familiar with a meditation, adapt it as you see fit.

Chapter 5

Friend, Enemy, Stranger

The foundation of equilibrium meditation is to see how senseless and disadvantageous it is for us to make such distinctions. The attitudes of hatred, attachment and close-minded ignorance that arise in us when we view others in terms of these fixed labels are highly detrimental to ourselves and others.

Lama Yeshe and Lama Zopa Rinpoche, *Wisdom Energy*

THE MEDITATION

Begin by recognizing that you are in the presence of God and asking God for the grace to develop love and compassion toward all people.

Imagine three people in front of you: someone you like and regard as a friend, someone you are not on good terms with (for shorthand, an "enemy"), and someone to whom you are indifferent (a "stranger"). Call to mind a particular person for each category: a good friend to whom you feel very close and for whom you have great affection; someone you don't like or who has done something to harm you; and someone you don't really know, a person for whom you feel no emotion, perhaps someone you see on the bus or train in the morning or whom you pass on the street on your way to school or work.

Take the time to allow a clear and firm picture of each of these three individuals to form in your mind. You want to be able to retain the image of these three persons throughout the meditation.

Start by focusing on the friend. Allow your feelings for this friend to arise. Really allow yourself to experience all of your positive feelings of love and friendship toward this person. It may help to think of a specific wonderful experience you had with this person, perhaps a recent visit during which the two of you really connected.

As you revel in the feelings of friendship, notice how solid your conviction of this person as "friend" is, how definitively you view him or her as "friend." When you are immersed in your positive feeling for the person, the person seems concretely to be your friend. As you notice the concreteness of the category, be aware how much you want this person to be happy.

Now shift your focus to the enemy. Allow your feelings for this person to arise. Without judgment or embarrassment, really let yourself experience all of the negative feelings you have toward this person, whether they take the form of dislike, repulsion, anger, disappointment, or some other emotion you regard as negative. Perhaps part of the feeling that arises is hurt caused by something this person has done to you.

As you experience these negative feelings, notice how solid your conviction of this person as "enemy" is. When you are immersed in your negative feelings, the person seems concretely to be someone at odds with you. Carefully note your feelings toward the person. Be aware of how unimportant this person's happiness is to you.

Finally, shift your focus to the stranger, and note your feeling of indifference (which you may experience as a lack of any feeling) toward the person. Sit in that feeling of indifference, noticing the solidity of both the feeling and the label of stranger.

Next spend some time reflecting on the basis on which you put each of these three persons into the category that you did, the basis on which you label one a friend, another an enemy, and the third a stranger. Starting with your friend, consider what it is that causes you to label this person as your friend. Notice how much of your feeling about the person is generated by the fact that the person does or says things that make you feel good, that satisfy your needs and desires.

Now do the same with the enemy and then with the stranger. Notice how much your label for each depends on what the person does or doesn't do for you.

In fact, notice how much of the label depends on what the person does or doesn't do *now*, at this particular time in the relationship (or lack of relationship in the case of the stranger). Focusing on your friend, try to remember a time when the person was not your friend. Perhaps you didn't like the person or were indifferent toward him or her when you first met. Remember that the person was not always your friend, that there was a time when you were not friends.

Now imagine a situation that might cause the friendship to change or end. Really put yourself in a situation where the person you label friend might behave unfeelingly toward you or do something that hurts you, something that feels like your friend is turning against you. Allow yourself to experience the hurt and bad feelings that would result from this. When you do, what happens to the warm feelings you had toward that person? What happens to your desire for him or her to be happy? How solid does the label "friend" feel when you do this?

When you feel some loosening of the solidity of the label, recognize that relationships change. Today's friend was not always and may not always be a friend. Therefore, there is no good reason for picking out the person you currently label as friend as uniquely deserving of your love and kindness.

Next put your focus on the enemy. First, recall that there was a time when you did not have negative feelings toward this person. Try to remember, if you can, your initial reactions toward the person or some earlier period in your relationship when your feelings toward the person were softer than they are now. Isn't it the case that you did not always consider the person an enemy?

Now imagine something that might change the negative way you currently regard the person you label as enemy. Really allow yourself to imagine a scenario where this might happen—perhaps the person performing an unexpected kindness to you or the discovery that the two of you share an unsuspected common interest. It might help if you can recall a situation where someone with whom you were on bad terms did something that caused the relationship between you to improve. As you allow the scenario to unfold, be attentive to your feelings. As you consider the person, notice how your negative feelings toward the person soften.

When you feel some loosening of the solidity of the label, recognize that relationships change. Today's enemy was not always and may not always be enemy. Therefore, there is no good reason to withhold your feelings of love and kindness from this person.

Next put your focus on the stranger. Imagine how easy it is for someone to cease to be a stranger. A chance conversation. A kind word. Or perhaps an unkind one. It would take so little for the stranger to become friend or enemy. If that is the case, how can your feelings of indifference toward this person be solid? Just as the people you currently label friend or enemy were once strangers, so too this person so easily could become your best of friends or worst of enemies.

Now picture all three persons standing in front of you. Recognize that there is no permanence to the labels that you give to them. And that the differences in how you label these persons is based on a self-centered viewpoint, not on inherent and unchanging differences in the three people. Isn't it the case that if your conception of their qualities as friend, enemy, or stranger came from their side, that if the qualities were inherent in them and not a product of your perception, then the person would be friend, enemy, or stranger for everyone? Everyone would label the person as you do, wouldn't they? Yet they don't, do they? If the labels don't come from the person, how can you justify being attached to one, having aversion to another, and being indifferent toward the third?

Recognize that, just like you, each of these persons wants happiness and love. They are equal in wanting happiness and wanting to avoid suffering. And recognize that each of them has the capacity to develop love and compassion toward others. Recognize that each of these people shares the same divine nature; each one has been created by and is loved by God.

Now picture three persons standing before Jesus: his mother, the soldier who drove the nails into his hands, and someone who was in a crowd when he spoke, but to whom Jesus never spoke. Look at Jesus as he gazes at each of them. Notice how he has love and compassion toward each of them. See how he recognizes the suffering of each of them and wants to help them all, without distinction.

With Jesus' love in your mind, again picture your friend, enemy, and stranger. Allow the feelings of care and love and compassion that you have for your friend to expand to cover each of the three people in front of you. Feel your love and Jesus' love radiating out to cover first the three people in front of you and then to everyone else.

As you bring your contemplation to a close, spend some time in dialogue with Jesus about what you learned. If there were places you had difficulty, talk to Jesus about them. And listen to what he might want to convey to you.

COMMENTARY

In St. John's Gospel, Jesus gives his disciples a "new" commandment: love one another as I have loved you (Jn 13:34). Jesus' consistent teaching during his public ministry was that this is not a command to love only those it is easy to love. Rather, we are called to love everyone.

Jesus is quite explicit that his call is a call to universal love. In St. Matthew's Gospel, Jesus refers to the familiar saying "love your neighbor and hate your enemy" and counters it with the command to "love your enemies and pray for those who persecute you," in imitation of the God who "makes his sun rise on the bad and the good, and causes rain to fall on the just and the unjust." After all, says Jesus, it is no great challenge or meritorious act to love only those who love us; even the tax collectors do the same (Mt 5:43–46). In St. Luke's Gospel Jesus drives the point home with the story of the Good Samaritan, a story intended to teach that everyone is our "neighbor" (Lk 10:29–37).

This same universal compassion or love is a fundamental value of Buddhism. In the Sutta Nipata, Buddha says, "Just as a mother would protect her only child at the risk of her own life, even so, cultivate a boundless heart towards all beings. Let your thoughts of boundless love pervade the whole world." In Mahayana Buddhism, the bodhisattva ideal is to feel compassion for all sentient beings (human and nonhuman), and Buddhists strive to attain bodhicitta, the mind that cherishes others—*all* others without distinction—over the self. That includes those who have behaved badly to us; in words strikingly reminiscent of those of

Jesus in Matthew, the great eighth-century teacher Santideva wrote, "If you do not practice compassion toward your enemy then toward whom can you practice it?"[1] Thus Tibetan Buddhist thought, like Christian thought, encourages us to have equal regard for all other beings, regardless of whether they like us or don't like us, help us or don't help us, harm us or don't harm us. The difference is that Christians think of that universal love as extending to all human beings, those made in the image of God, whereas Buddhists look at all sentient beings as the objects of their compassion.

We have a natural tendency to discriminate in our feelings toward other persons. We either like, dislike, or are indifferent or neutral toward everyone we meet. Although we tend not to focus on this reality, those feelings are generally determined by how the other person behaves toward us; in Buddhist terms, our feelings toward others are based on greed/attachment and anger/aversion. Greed/attachment causes you to label as friend someone who is good to you or helps you and anger/aversion causes you to label as enemy those who disturb your happiness. So the label is not inherent in the other person, but stems from our own delusions. As Buddhist teachers always say, if the other person were truly inherently an enemy, everyone—even the Buddha—would view him as such. Instead, the same person I have warm, loving feelings toward may be despised by someone else; and a person I can't stand to spend time with is the best friend of another.

Not only is our usual approach self-centered, but we treat the qualities of others and the feelings they generate in us as permanent and unchanging. We act as though those we have labeled friends have always been our friends and will always remain our friends. We act as though those we have labeled enemies have always been and will always be enemies. We assume we will always feel close to the former and that we will never feel that way toward the latter. We don't even think about strangers, generally excluding them from our locus of concern altogether.

All you have to do is examine your own experience to know that these assumptions are mistaken. We've all experienced relationships that change. People we were once close to no longer are. People we once regarded with indifference or did not particularly like become friends. We change. Other people change. Situations change. And that means that a person's status as our friend, enemy, or stranger changes. The enemy of last year may be friend of this year; the friend of this morning can be enemy in the afternoon; one smile can turn a stranger into a friend.

Lama Thubten Zopa Rinpoche talked about the strangeness of the fact that we make our determinations of whether someone is a friend or enemy based on "the nearest action." In his example, someone gives you one thousand dollars in the morning and in the afternoon kicks you. Because of that last act, in your mind, he is enemy. Yet, why do we count the nearest action as important? Why don't we refer back to past actions? If you think about it, there is no reason that we make our determination based on the last action, yet we do have that tendency. It is as though the closest-in-time act negates everything that came before it. (We tend to do the same thing as a society in terms of how we judge public figures.) Lama Zopa explained that because we regard the happiness of each moment as so important, even if someone has benefited us in the past, if he does something now that harms us or otherwise disturbs our current happiness, we view him negatively. We label him as an enemy now regardless of what he did in the past. Thus, anger and other bad feelings toward the person easily arise.

The purpose of the *Friend, Enemy, Stranger* meditation for the Christian is the same as it is for a Tibetan Buddhist: to help counter our tendency to discriminate in our attitudes toward others. The aim is to eliminate attachment to some and aversion or lack of concern toward others. Because that kind of nondiscriminating love, especially toward those who do not behave in a loving manner toward us, is not something that can be forced as a matter of the will, meditative practices like this one are very useful. If we can come to a deep realization that our perceptions of a person as inherently a friend or inherently an enemy are flawed—that there is no inherent friend or inherent enemy, just arbitrary, mistaken, and changeable labels we put on people based on our own selfish motivations, it is easier to cultivate equanimity. Equanimity does not mean there will not be some people we feel closer to than others; that is natural. What we seek is an equal concern and regard for all others, regardless of whether they help or harm us.

A word about labels. Almost every time I have taught this meditation, someone says to me, "I don't have any enemies." It is true that many, if not most, of us don't have people whom we actually label enemies. But I daresay all of us have people we view as difficult, people we have some aversion to. All of us know people whom, either because of something they have done to us (or to someone we love) or because they have some personal characteristic that is displeasing to us, we don't like. Think of the term "enemy" as simply shorthand for people who generate negative reactions in you, whatever the specific nature of those negative reactions. Likewise, the term "friend" does not have to mean your closest friend, merely someone for whom it is easy for you to generate positive feelings.

I made several adaptations to the *Friend, Enemy, Stranger* meditation as I first learned it as a Buddhist. First, because Buddhists believe in reincarnation, and Tibetans speak of our having lived "beginningless lives," when Buddhists do this meditation, they begin by considering that because they have lived countless lives, they can't assume that the person who is a friend now was a friend in a past life, or that the enemy now was an enemy in a past life. The idea is to realize that given that we have lived countless lives, every person has been the best of friends and the worst of enemies. I obviously leave that part out here, an omission that is not of great consequence. Christians and others who do not believe in reincarnation have experienced enough change in their feelings toward others to be able to engage in the contemplation based only on experiences in this human life.

Apart from leaving out the consideration of past lives, the adaptations I made occur at the beginning and near the end of the meditation. I invite you to begin the meditation by asking God for the grace to develop love and compassion toward all people. St. Ignatius, in whose tradition I was trained as a spiritual director, recommended that we begin all of our periods of prayer by asking God for the grace we seek in that prayer time. He taught that this disposes us to recognize our need for God and helps to focus our mind. Thus, I often include the step of asking for grace in these meditations, something that also reminds us that our contemplation here is something we are doing with God, not something we are doing on our own. Even in meditations where I don't include this step, you can add it yourself.

In order to aid us in the gradual development of equanimity toward all, I include near the end of the meditation, first, a recognition of the divine creation of each human person and, then, a visualization of Jesus. Reminding ourselves that Jesus loved and had compassion toward all of those with whom he came in contact—not only those, like his mother, who were "good" disciples, but also those who tortured and put him to death—is helpful in our own development of such expansive love and compassion.

My final adaptation is the recommendation to end the meditation with what St. Ignatius called a colloquy, a conversation with Jesus. Think of it as talking with Jesus about what just happened in the meditation—what did I learn? Where did I struggle? Based on what I experienced, how do I need Jesus to be with me? The colloquy is an important dynamic of Ignatian prayer and it is a useful way to end any type of prayer exercise. If is it new to you, you may feel a bit self-conscious at first. However, my experience has been that most people who do engage in the practice for some time respond very positively to it and find themselves more open to "hearing" God's response in whatever form that may take.

It will take some time, but we can gradually move beyond the self-centered way in which we evaluate others and learn to feel compassion for all and wish for the well-being of all. It has also been my experience, and the experience of others, that this meditation can help in dealing with resentment toward a particular person.

As a postscript, although the point of this particular exercise is to soften our labels of people as friend, enemy, or stranger, we should be aware that we label people in all sorts of ways and that those labels have an effect. Lama Thubten Zopa Rinpoche used the example of someone who has never before seen a Tibetan lama, but who has encountered Hare Krishnas, who also have shaved heads and wear robes. When that person sees a Tibetan lama for the first time, he mentally labels the person he sees as a Hare Krishna and "believes in what he labels. The person is Hare Krishna to him." When he asks the monk if he is a Hare Krishna, he learns for the first time that the person is a Tibetan Buddhist monk. Now he mentally labels the person a Tibetan Buddhist monk. "The person stops labeling the monk a Hare Krishna, so Hare Krishna stops appearing to the person's mind. In its place is the appearance of a Tibetan monk. What appears to you is what you have labeled."[2]

Once we give a person a label, the label defines how the person appears to us. Perhaps an added benefit of this meditation will be a greater awareness of all the labels we employ and the effect of those labels.

Chapter 6

Sending and Taking (Tong-len)

*Although at present we do not have the ability to reach and benefit
all beings, it is our responsibility to develop our minds so that we
completely change the self-cherishing attitude into one of helping
and cherishing others.*

Geshe Rabten and Geshe Dhargyey,
Advice from a Spiritual Friend

THE MEDITATION

Begin by recalling that you are in the presence of God, who
breathes life into you in each moment. Spend a few minutes
focusing on the life-giving breath that comes in and out of your
body. Each time you inhale, feel God's love and light being drawn
into your body. With each exhalation, feel all of your anxieties and
concerns leaving your body.

As you breathe in and out, it may help to visualize God in
whatever form brings you most directly in touch with God's compassion and love for you. It might be the Sacred Heart of Jesus or
Jesus as the Good Shepherd. With that image in mind, continue
to breathe in God's love and light in the form of white light coming from your visualized image of God. Continue to breathe out
your anxieties and concerns.

After you have done this for several minutes, visualize in front
of you someone for whom you have great love and concern who is

suffering from some physical, mental, or emotional illness. Let it be a person you know who is suffering and whom you care about and wish to help. Bring that person and his or her suffering clearly into focus. Let your natural feelings of love and compassion for the person rise. Allow yourself to feel your desire to help relieve the person's suffering.

As you sit with the image of the person before you, visualize the cause of the suffering taking the form of black smoke pervading the person's being. See the black smoke circulating throughout the person's body.

Now, as you inhale, visualize the black smoke being pulled from the person into your body, as you see yourself taking on the other person's suffering. Really let yourself see and feel the cause of the person's pain and suffering moving from his or her body to your own—as though you were taking a heavy load from the other person. Take the suffering in sincerely and with concentration.

As you exhale, visualize your breath in the form of white light passing from you to the other person, white light through which you send to the other person love, happiness, and whatever would relieve the person's suffering. Watch as the black smoke leaving the person's body is replaced by the white light that you send.

Continue to inhale and exhale—inhaling the pain and the cause of suffering in the form of black smoke and exhaling love and healing in the form of white light.

If you feel yourself flinching or hesitating as you inhale, recall that God is with you. Ask for God's strength and support to help you alleviate the other person's suffering.

If you continue to feel hesitation, it might help to see yourself as a conduit of God's love and healing: Visualize the white light you are sending out as you exhale flowing through you from God. Visualize the black smoke that you take in as you inhale passing through your heart and moving down through your feet before dissolving into the ground. As it passes through your heart, let it take with it all of your feelings of selfishness and self-cherishing. Along with the suffering from the other person, those feelings pass down through your feet and dissolve into the ground.

Continue inhaling and exhaling like this for some period of time.

When you feel ready to move on, reflect on all of the suffering that exists in the world around you. Let your mind wander over all of the causes of suffering of human beings everywhere—wars, violence, mental and physical illnesses, poverty, natural disasters, and so forth. Let a kaleidoscope of images of the suffering of the world present itself to you. As the images pass before you, notice that there is no one who does not experience suffering in one form or another. Some people suffer more than others, but everyone experiences some form of suffering.

As you visualize all of the suffering of so many people in the world, feel how good it would be if you could do something to alleviate the pain of others, if you could do something to make their lives less painful.

Now visualize in front of you, standing with the person who has been the object of your practice, all of the people of your community (your school, work, or parish community). Generate toward those people the feeling of love you have for the person you have been praying with. Feel toward them the same desire that they be freed from their suffering.

As you inhale, take in the source of their pain in the form of black smoke. Take it in sincerely and with concentration from all directions. As you exhale, visualize your breath in the form of white light going forth in all directions, sending healing love to everyone it touches. Continue to inhale and exhale.

Again if you feel yourself hesitating as you inhale, remind yourself that you are not alone—that God is with you—and ask

God for strength and support as you seek to alleviate the suffering of others. Remember that you are a conduit of God's love and healing.

After continuing the practice for some period of time, broaden your focus. Visualize all of the suffering people of the world in front of you. Generate toward all of them the feeling of love you have already generated for the person you began the practice with and those in your community. Feel toward them the same desire that they be freed from their suffering.

As you inhale, take in the source of their pain in the form of black smoke. Take it in sincerely and with concentration from all directions. As you exhale, visualize your breath in the form of white light going forth in all directions, sending healing love to everyone it touches. Continue to inhale and exhale.

Notice your own feelings as you engage in the practice. If there is a specific suffering you are experiencing—loneliness, some physical pain, fear—generate the wish to relieve all people of that particular suffering. Visualize yourself taking in that form of suffering from all people, and send out healing white light to all of them.

Again, be attentive to any feeling of hesitation at taking in the suffering, asking for God's strength and reminding yourself that you are not alone, but are a conduit of God's love and healing.

Engage in the practice for as long as you wish. As you draw your prayer to a close, generate the strong desire that your meditation be the cause of alleviating the suffering of others in the world.

End the meditation with a period of colloquy—spend some time talking to God about what you have experienced. Be sure to spend time focusing with God on the sources of your hesitation in taking on the suffering of others. With God by your side, look at the hesitation from all sides. If you can, try to understand where the hesitation comes from and what it feels like in your body. Talk with God about the fears that prevent you from being a fully open conduit of God's love and healing to others.

COMMENTARY

Tong-len is a Tibetan word meaning sending and taking, which perfectly describes the action of the meditation. The aim of the practice is to help us both to develop a different relationship to suffering and to deepen our compassion toward others.

Our usual approach to life is to seek pleasure and avoid suffering. We tend to go out of our way to avoid experiencing suffering. And, while very few of us would be comfortable putting it in these terms, our own comfort and freedom from suffering are generally more important to us than the comfort and freedom from suffering of others, with the exception of our children and perhaps a few others who are extraordinarily close to us. This meditation invites us to consciously abandon our normal tendencies by willingly taking on the suffering of others. In so doing, we try to free ourselves from the self-cherishing mind that prefers our own well-being to that of others.

From a Buddhist perspective, the practice of tong-len emulates the bodhisattva ideal of self-sacrifice, the willingness to take on the suffering of others. It is a wonderful meditation to adapt for Christians, since working for the well-being of others is as fundamental in Christianity as it is in Mahayana Buddhism.

As Christians, our model is Jesus, the supreme example of self-sacrifice and cherishing others over self. Throughout the Gospels Jesus performs many miracles of healing, showing his compassion for the suffering of others. At the Last Supper, he offers his disciples the cup "which is poured out for you" as the new covenant in his blood (Lk 22:20). In John's Gospel, Jesus washes the feet of the disciples, taking on the role of a lowly servant (Jn 13:5–20). Afterward, he offers the ultimate sacrifice, giving his life out of love for us. Jesus' actions are a model for our own behavior. The idea is not for us to sit back and admire Jesus for his selflessness, enjoying the benefit of what he suffered for us, but rather that we conform our behavior to his. "If anyone serves Me he must follow Me," Jesus tells his disciples (Jn 12:26). "Take up [your] cross daily and follow Me," he instructs (Lk 9:23). After washing the disciples' feet at the Last Supper, Jesus tells them, "For I gave you an example that you also should do as I did to you" (Jn 13:15).

In India and Nepal I learned several different ways to do the tong-len practice. It is generally recommended to begin the practice focusing on a parent or other relative, someone for whom it is easy for you to feel great love and concern, and then to gradually expand the circle of persons included in the practice. It is easier to overcome selfishness with respect to a person whom we love deeply than with respect to nameless crowds of suffering people. We are willing to do extraordinary things to try to alleviate the suffering of those we love. Here, we willingly take on their suffering for the sake of their healing. Some people, however, find it too painful to do the practice with someone to whom they are very close, someone they love a great deal, especially if the person is suffering from a grave illness. If you find that to be the case when you've tried the practice a couple of times, try the meditation instead with someone who is less immediate to you, but still someone of whom you have personal knowledge and whom you regard with affection, perhaps the sick parent or sibling of a friend.

No matter whom you choose, it is important to make it real. For the meditation to have the greatest effect, it is important to envision a specific person experiencing a particular suffering. If you don't have a real, specific suffering in mind that you are taking in, it is much harder to generate a true reaction. Similar advice holds when you shift from focusing on one individual to visualizing the suffering of all people: try to keep it real and specific. Don't envision a faceless mass of people, but try to see the faces of actual individuals with real and identifiable sufferings. This should not be difficult; most of us are personally aware of so many people who suffer in one way or another.

Make no mistake: doing this practice seriously is challenging. If you truly visualize yourself taking on the suffering of another, you will feel some fear, some hesitation. The thought might arise, "If I assume all the sufferings and the problems of others, I won't be able to bear it" or simply, "I don't want to experience this suffering."

Several adaptations I made to this meditation have the effect of addressing the hesitations and fears that tend to arise. First is the invitation to call directly on God's assistance, which will be easier for you if you begin the meditation by developing a firm sense of God's presence. Second, I encourage seeing yourself at the outset breathing with the breath of God, calling forth our Christian understanding that God breathes life into each of us every moment, that God sustains us with every breath we take. Being conscious of the connection between your breath and God's helps set the stage for the "channel" image, which can be very helpful. When we are at our best in channeling God and God's love, there is no limit to either what we give or what we can take. If I can truly see myself as a channel, what flows through me to others is God's love, which is limitless. But if I believe it is just me alone taking in the black smoke, it is quite understandable that there will be fear and concern that I will reach a saturation point; I am finite and can hold only so much. If, however, I receive as a channel of God, there is no saturation point, because I'm acting as

God's instrument, taking in for God, and letting the suffering flow through me and dissipate, leaving room only for God's love.

In a similar vein, I also made an adaptation to the meditation regarding what happens to the black smoke. Buddhist instructions for this meditation often suggest that the practitioner let the black smoke dissolve into the core of the ego. One instruction I received was to take in suffering in the form of dark fog that becomes a great thunderbolt that strikes and destroys the false conception of the self that causes self-cherishing. I modify that suggestion for two reasons. First, that instruction is given so that the Buddhist meditation on compassion becomes a form of meditation on emptiness. My goal in this meditation, however, is to keep the focus on developing compassion and cherishing of others. Second, the Buddhist method of doing the meditation focuses on the individual alone as the source of destruction of the ego, whereas as a Christian I wish to underscore that we are working with God.

Even with the assistance of God, the practice may seem difficult at first. However, if you continue to engage in it, you will learn to recognize that thoughts like "I can't take on this suffering" or "I can't bear it" are only self-cherishing thoughts that have no basis in reality. The thoughts may continue to arise—indeed, they likely will—but when they do, you will over time more easily recognize them as having no basis in reality.

This tong-len practice can be done for people who are ill or dying, or who are experiencing any kind of pain or suffering. Although here I give instruction for doing it as part of a prayer session, once you become accustomed to the practice, it is possible to do it at any time. So, for example, if you are driving on the road and see an accident, you can begin to breathe in the suffering of any injured people and send out healing light to them. Or if you are walking and see an angry couple who are arguing bitterly, you can breathe in their anger and send forth healing love. Think how much better it would be to engage in this practice than to see suffering and look away in fear, discomfort, or confusion. The basic idea is simple—breathe in suffering and breathe out love, compassion, and healing—and can be adapted to any situation.

There are other variations you can make to the meditation. First, if you are experiencing serious physical, mental, or emotional pain, you can spend an entire prayer period engaged simply in the introductory portion of the meditation—breathing in God's love and healing in the form of white light and breathing out your pain in the form of black smoke. Again, once you have developed some familiarity with the practice, you can do this any time you are experiencing stress or pain—whether you are driving, sitting in your office, at home, or any other place.

Second, particularly when dealing with the suffering of a person very close to you, you can imagine holding the person in your arms as you breathe in and out. Visualize the person sitting on your lap, leaning into your chest with your arms around him or her as you engage in the practice, so that you are breathing directly into the person. I have found this to be extremely powerful when praying with the suffering of very close friends.

Both Buddhists and Christians recognize that the goal is not to alleviate just the physical suffering of others, but their spiritual suffering as well. From a Buddhist perspective, the ultimate aim is to bring all sentient beings to a state of Enlightenment. From a Christian perspective, it is to help others attain union with God. When Jesus healed people, the physical healing was symbolic of his forgiveness of their sins and of his desire to restore their relationship with God. As you do the meditation, try to be aware of that distinction, holding a broad view of the suffering you are trying to alleviate and recognizing that you are concerned with more than the other person's present suffering.

I have been asked what the point of this practice is, or how it could have any effect on the person who is the subject of the prayer. These are understandable questions. As seen in the quote with which I opened this chapter, even Tibetan teachers acknowledge that "ordinary beings" do not have the power to actually take away the suffering of others.

Although some people do believe that the practice has actual effect, its real value does not lie in what it does or does not do to the object of the meditation. The Dalai Lama, who has recommended this practice, said that while it is difficult to assess the benefit of tong-len to others, it is clearly of benefit to the person who engages in it. If you engage in this practice strongly and purely, the intention or thought of exchanging self for others will come more easily. It helps generate more strongly a mind that cherishes others and a deep desire to alleviate their suffering. The development of such a mind-set helps us better to meet the material and spiritual needs of others. Sogyal Rinpoche, a great lama in the Nyingma tradition of Tibetan Buddhism, says of tong-len, "No other practice I know is as effective in destroying the self-grasping, self-cherishing, self-absorption of the ego."[1]

When I suggest that at the end of the meditation you should generate a strong desire that your meditation be the cause of alleviating the suffering of others in the world, I do not intend to suggest a direct causal link between your breath and another's healing. But the spiritual growth you achieve by doing the practice enables you to be a better conduit of God's love and healing presence in the world.

Chapter 7

The Kindness of Others

*Whenever we see or think about our mother—or someone else who
has taken exceptional care of us—there is an automatic recognition of
who she is, and a certain strong feeling arises within us.... Thinking
first about the mother of our present life is the best way to progress
in our development of bodhicitta.*

Lama Yeshe and Lama Thubten Zopa

Rinpoche, *Wisdom Energy*

THE MEDITATION

Begin by recognizing that you are in the presence of God and
asking God for the grace to develop gratitude and love toward all
people.

Consider the kindness of your mother. Think of the way she
took care of herself while you were in her womb...how much of
her bodily energy went into nurturing you before you were
born...how much she loved you even then. Form in your mind a
picture of her during those months, carrying you like a precious
jewel. Really experience all that she did for you and how she felt
toward you.

Now imagine the physical pain your mother went through
giving birth to you. Even though she may have suffered great pain,
picture how unconcerned she was about that pain, caring only
that you be born healthy, and excited about your arrival.

Then consider how your mother cared for you while you were an infant requiring so much attention. She thought of you twenty-four hours a day, often going without sleep to take care of you. In your mind, picture her holding you. Really allow yourself to feel what that felt like.

Next reflect on all the things she did for you as you grew. Made sure you got a good education. Helped you with your homework and taught you things outside of school. Comforted and cared for you when you were sick. Reassured you when you were frightened. Go back through your memories, seeing how much she was there for you and how much she sacrificed to take care of you.

Try to develop a deep sense of the kindness of your mother, of how much of who you are and what you have is the result of her kindness toward you during your formative years.

Now consider how even in your adult life, your mother is there for you. Realize how much you take for granted all the many kind things your mother does for you. Or if your mother has died, look back on all the things she did for you during your adult life before her death.

After spending time reflecting on the kindness of your own mother, consider the kindness of others toward you. Begin by considering the kindness of other family members—your father, aunts and uncles, grandparents, older siblings. Look back at incidents where one or another of them was there for you, giving you the emotional, physical, or spiritual support that you needed. Let the incidents pass before your mind, as though you were riding in a boat on a moving stream, gliding past an ever-changing shoreline. As you watch, let yourself realize how kind these family members have been to you.

Now do the same with your teachers and other mentors. Go back over the events of your past, picturing your interactions with them and catching glimpses of their kindness toward you.

Next broaden your consideration to the other people you come in contact with during the course of your day. Review the events of an entire recent day. See how much you have benefited from the kindness of others. Reflect on the extent to which you are dependent on other people for food, clothing, housing, medicine, in short, all of the things you need to survive. Think about the breakfast or lunch you had today. How many people had a hand in that food sitting before you? The farmers who tilled the fields, the laborers who harvested, the packagers and shippers. Consider how many people were involved.

Do the same with the clothes you are wearing. The bed you sleep in. The house you live in. All of the other products you use and consume. Everything you have has been touched by another person. Everything you have comes by the labor and kindness of another person.

Now realize that it is not only your friends and people who are good to you that you depend on. Even those you have difficulty with benefit you greatly by giving you the occasion to practice patience and generosity. Hear Jesus reminding you that there is no merit in loving those who love you or doing good to those who do good to you. Even those you find most difficult are an inestimable aid to your spiritual growth. Allow yourself to realize that there is no one who has not in one way or another provided some benefit to you.

What is your response to this kindness? As you feel the gratitude arise toward all those who have shown you such kindness, realize that the only possible grateful response is to repay the kindness of those who have been so very good to you. How can you do that?

Picture Jesus as your model. Reflect on the events of his public ministry, especially on how he showed love to all and how no one was beyond the reach of his compassion.

Consider that Jesus shows us a way to repay the kindness of others. We can do that by accepting his invitation to each of us to be Christ to others, to convey the love and kindness of Christ to them.

Now reflect on the fact that what really benefits others is helping them to achieve ultimate happiness, to help bring them to a state of greater union with God. Develop a sense that it is your responsibility to help them to achieve this. Wouldn't failure to do so be like failing to help a blind person in danger of walking over a precipice?

As you bring your meditation to an end, talk to Jesus about the gratitude you feel for having received so much kindness from other people and ask him to help you find ways to repay that kindness. Ask Jesus to show you how to be more like him, how to love as expansively as he does.

COMMENTARY

Tibetan Buddhist teaching recognizes that some people's motivation for attaining Enlightenment is simply to end their own suffering. However, for the Tibetan Buddhist the ultimate goal is to achieve bodhicitta—the mind that cherishes others over the self and wishes to obtain Enlightenment for the sake of all sentient beings, all who experience the suffering of the cycle of birth and rebirth, human and nonhuman. This is considered the highest level of motivation for Enlightenment. It is viewed as unbecoming to selfishly work only for your own welfare, neglecting the welfare of others.

The meditation on recognizing the kindness of others is designed to help overcome selfishness. The idea is that reflecting on the kindness shown us by others helps us develop a universal love and compassion and thus the desire to work for more than our own happiness. The hope is that recognition of the kindness of others helps generate willingness to actively work on their behalf and bring them happiness. Thus, the aim of the original Tibetan analytical meditation is to cultivate the wish to obtain Enlightenment for the sake of all other sentient beings.

The mother is used as the primary object of meditation because the love of a mother for her child is viewed as a key way to understand and to generate universal compassion and loving kindness. The idea is to take the loving and grateful response that spontaneously arises toward this person, who has shown us such unconditional love and cared for us so solicitously, and extend it to all beings.

The meditation is particularly easily adaptable for Christians. First, regardless of what religion we follow, we are all equally dependent on other beings for our survival. Every good thing that we have depends on the work of others. As one lama said, even honeybees with no intelligence understand their dependence on others. Christians recognize that all we have and all we are comes from God, but we also recognize our interdependence with other human beings and the extent to which we rely on them.

Related to that, an emphasis on gratitude is no less a part of the Christian than the Buddhist tradition. Developing a sense of gratitude can go a long way toward overcoming our selfishness. With reference to this meditation, Geshe Rabten writes, "since sentient beings have been very kind to us and are in a miserable situation, it is unworthy to forget about them and be concerned only with ourself. . . . We should try to abandon our selfish attitude and, remembering the kindness of other sentient beings, try to use our entire existence, our body, speech and mind, in order to benefit them. This is the attitude of repaying the kindness."[1] Lama Yeshe and Lama Zopa suggest that we "become like the dutiful child who takes on the responsibility of helping his mother through difficult times. We cannot bear the thought that others must face their incredible suffering."[2]

Finally, meditating on the love of a mother is eminently suitable for Christians. Just as Tibetan Buddhists view the love of a mother for her child as possessing particular significance, motherly love has a special place in Christian theology. We have numerous biblical images of God as mother, as in Isaiah, where God promises that "as one whom a mother comforts, so I will comfort you" (Is 66:13). We have the image of Mary, Christ's mother, as our mother and we see numerous artistic representations of Mary cradling the baby Jesus or supporting the crucified Jesus. Oscar Romero observed that "Mothers are like the sacrament of God's love. The Arabs say that God, who we are unable to see, created the mother who we are able to see—and in all mothers we see God, we see love, we see tenderness."[3]

The mother image operates a little differently in the Buddhist context, and I have adapted the meditation accordingly. Because they believe in reincarnation, Tibetan Buddhists teach that all sentient beings have been our mother in one lifetime or another. As a result, when they do the meditation, after considering the kindness of the mother in this life, they consider (a) that this is not the first lifetime in which the present mother has been mother and (b) that each other sentient being, in one lifetime or another, has been as kind to us as our present mother has been. Thus, for Tibetan Buddhists, the effectiveness of this meditation is strengthened by the conviction that we are subject to rebirth and have lived countless lives.

The adapted meditation, in which I (for the obvious reason) leave out the consideration of past lives, is based on the idea of carrying forward the love of the mother as we consider the kindness of others toward us. From a Catholic perspective, the idea of the love of the mother as a paradigm for all of our human relationships is a natural one. In Catholic thought, the institution of family is central. The family gives us our first revelation of our connectedness to others, teaching us that we are born into a covenantal relationship with others. The covenant, however, does not exist merely among family members. Rather, the family is the paradigm for all human relationships; it is the blueprint for our relation to the broader human community. Thus the process of extension in this meditation should be natural for Christians.

Because Christians believe humans are made in God's image, the meditation speaks only of a desire to relieve other humans of their suffering, rather than the broader Buddhist goal of relieving the suffering of all sentient beings.

Finally, because Jesus is the embodiment of God's universal love and compassion and therefore our model for developing that love and compassion, I've added to the meditation an invitation to reflect on how Jesus conducted himself during his life. Part of our aim as Christians is to see through Jesus' eyes, to try to see everyone as he did. We always want to remember that the universal love and compassion we seek is God's unlimited love for all of God's children—that all persons are created in the image of God and God loves them equally.

For both Buddhists and Christians the desire to repay the kindness of others is a desire not to meet simply their material needs but their spiritual ones as well. For a Buddhist this means bringing others to Enlightenment. For a Christian it means living in the hope and desire to help lead others to Christ. We desire to see Christ in others and that they see Christ in us.

Let me note one potential stumbling block, something that creates difficulties for some people in doing this meditation. Many people have strained relationships with their mothers (something that appears to be more common among Westerners than among

Tibetans). Tibetan teachers of this meditation recognize that some people's mothers have treated them badly and that they have strained relationships (to say the least). The traditional advice is to do the meditation thinking only of the positive side of the relationship with your mother, completely disregarding any unpleasant aspects; to ignore faults and pay attention only to good qualities. I think this can work for people who have strained or somewhat difficult relationships with their mothers; it is much less likely to be effective for those who have suffered abuse of one form or another at the hands of their mother. The advice is also easier for Buddhists, who believe in reincarnation and who therefore can recognize that even if the mother in this lifetime was unkind, they have had loving mothers in previous lifetimes. The mother who is unkind in this lifetime may have been very loving in another. That strategy is not available for Christians. Thus, some people will find the practice of this meditation as I present it very difficult.

Someone who finds it impossible to use the mother as the object of meditation can instead use the kindness of a brother or sister as the primary object of the meditation. We can generate feelings for our siblings—toward whom, even when we are on bad terms with them, we feel a natural love and compassion—and use them as a way of grounding our compassion for all other beings. If you have a particularly strong bond of love with your father, you could use him as the primary object. Whomever you use as the object, it is important to generate a strong feeling of gratitude for all that person has done for you.

Westerners also sometimes have difficulty in this meditation because they don't view the mother's care for her child as a kindness. Some feel that the mother is doing no more than her duty. It is, of course, true that those who bring a child into the world bear responsibility for it. We know that many people do not accept that responsibility gracefully, however, and so we should recognize with gratitude the kindness our mother showed in taking care of us.

In addition to motivating them to repay others' kindness by working on their behalf, many people find that this meditation has the effect of making them happier and more relaxed. You doubtless know from your own experience how much more relaxed your mind is when your focus is directed toward the well-being of another than when it is focused on your own. The peacefulness of your mind and the loving kindness you carry for others then has the potential to affect everyone around you in a positive way.

Chapter 8

Exchanging Self and Others

If you check your everyday life, you find that all obstacles, all undesirable experiences and failures, come from the selfish attitude.... If the selfish attitude is strong, bigger and bigger problems come, one after another.

Lama Thubten Zopa Rinpoche, *Perfect Freedom*

THE MEDITATION

Begin by reflecting on the kindness of others as in *The Kindness of Others* meditation.

Consider the ways in which you have been selfish, overly concerned with yourself. Go through the events of the past day or several days and note all of the instances where you considered your own comfort over that of others, dwelt on your own suffering—even when it was relatively minor—over the suffering of others. Consider everything, including incidents as minor as rushing to be the first in line at the cafeteria or not letting another car merge in front of you in traffic.

Next, visualize yourself standing before you on your left. On the right, imagine all of the other people living in the world today—countless numbers of individuals. Hold both images in front of you—your vision of yourself and your vision of the billions of other human beings who inhabit this planet, stretching out much farther than the eye can see.

Think about how much you want everyone to be good to you and how painful it is when they are not, how much pain you suffer when someone shows anger toward you or is unkind to you.

Call to mind a time in the recent past when someone has shown anger or behaved badly toward you. Really allow the situation to arise in your mind, replaying it in your head. Let yourself feel the pain that it caused you.

Now look again at all the others standing before you. Is there any difference between you and them? In terms of wanting happiness and the desire to avoid suffering, aren't they just like you? Just as you want happiness, don't all of them? Just as you feel pain when you are treated badly, don't they as well? Just as you feel you deserve to be happy and free from suffering, don't they feel that also? Is their "right" to obtain happiness and avoid suffering any less than yours?

Look at all of them again. Recognize that each one of them is created by the same God. Each of them is created in the image of God and shares in the divine nature of our God.

Hold in your mind the image of yourself on one side and all those others on the other side. No matter how important you are (however you define importance), you are only one single person and no matter how unimportant any of the others may be, they are so numerous you can't even comprehend the number.

Wouldn't an unbiased third person looking at the scene before you naturally see that the many are more important than the one? When you stand in the shoes of an unbiased third person looking at yourself and the others, isn't it clear that collectively they are more important than you?

Consider: is it right that all others should be used for the attainment of happiness for one, or should the one be used for the attainment of happiness for the others? What can you conclude, except that it is right for you to work for the happiness of all of those countless others?

Think about it in terms of others' treatment of you and your treatment of them. Even if everyone you come in contact with is angry with you and harms you, you are just one person. Even if the whole world criticizes and mistreats you, you are only one person.

In contrast, if you—one person—are unable to control your anger, for example, untold numbers of persons are harmed. Your anger affects everyone in your family, your workplace, everyone you come in contact with. Think of examples where your anger has caused harm to others—times, for example, when something you said or did colored the experience of a room full of people.

If you look at history, you can think of examples where one person's inability to control his anger has led to acts that have caused great harm. Think of examples of where the act of one individual had a detrimental effect on an enormous number of people. Consider how much harm would not have been done if that person had been able to master his anger.

Recognize that the possibility of anger exists in you. That even if you are not angry now, you have been angry in the past and situations will arise where that anger could return unless you engage in efforts to transform your mind—to put on the mind of Christ. Given the potential negative impact of one person's anger, recognize how important it is to spend time growing in your Christ-nature.

And it is not just anger, is it? The same analysis applied to anger also holds true of our selfish mind and the importance of growing in our love and cherishing of others. Consider examples in which the selfishness of one individual has an effect on the lives of many people. Perhaps you can think of occasions when your own selfishness has had a ripple effect on others.

On the other side, think of examples when the kindness or goodness of one person had a tremendous impact on the lives of a number of other people. What about situations in which your own kindness has had a significant effect?

Think of how much the happiness of others depends on you—on whether you are kind, smile at another, give some benefit to another, and so on.

Hold again in your mind the image of yourself on one side and all those others on the other side. What do you feel as you hold that image? What conclusions do you draw? Sit with Jesus and talk to him about your experience.

COMMENTARY

In the Tibetan Buddhist tradition this meditation is often done as an adjunct or sequel to the Buddhist version of the meditation on the kindness of others adapted in chapter 7. You may want to try it both as a stand-alone meditation and in combination with the other meditation.

Tibetan Buddhist teaching emphasizes that from the moment of our birth each of us begins to form the selfish attitude that it is more important for us to be happy than for others. Our primary concern is to eliminate our own problems (which we tend to focus on and see as more important and more serious than the problems of others) and achieve happiness for ourselves. Although we usually don't say it out loud or even consciously admit it to ourselves, we operate with the underlying premise that we are more important than others; we cherish the self over others.

Tibetan Buddhism teaches that all of the undesirable acts we commit are rooted in our self-cherishing mind. Out of that selfishness we commit negative acts of body, speech, and mind that range from killing and stealing (crimes of which most of us are not guilty) to promoting ourselves at the expense of others or ignoring the needs of others (which most of us are guilty of, in one way or another). When we are not concerned with others, we deprive them of their peace, their happiness, and their material needs. The effects on them of our acts (or inaction) should not be diffi- cult for us to apprehend. Just as we are unhappy when others act in ways that bring us harm, others are unhappy when we act in ways that bring harm to them. Just as we are unhappy when others speak badly of us, others suffer when we speak badly of them.

When we think only of the self, not only do we create suffering in others, but we also cause suffering in ourselves. As the quotation from Lama Zopa at the outset of this chapter suggests, much of the suffering we experience stems from an attitude of selfishness. If we replace our selfishness with a mind that cherishes others, that does not give paramount importance to the self, we avoid the creation of pain; if our primary concern is for others, we will not wish to harm them and we also create greater happiness for our- selves. Lama Zopa explains that if your mind is full of compassion and loving kindness,

> even if everyone harms you, from your side you see everyone
> as a friend. With a mind of compassion, everyone is a friend,
> you feel close to everyone. With a heart of compassion and
> loving kindness, you see beauty in everyone, the way a mother
> sees her most beloved child. If one has loving kindness and
> bodhicitta, then even if one has no money, even if one is
> homeless and has to beg for every meal, there is still happi-
> ness and peace.[1]

In contrast, without such compassion and loving kindness, regardless of how much wealth, reputation, or power you possess, you experience no peace and no real joy. A mind habituated to being selfish and disliking problems sees everything through a lens of dissatisfaction.

Thus, from a Buddhist perspective, our root mistake is renouncing others and cherishing the self. By eliminating self-cherishing, by giving up the selfish attitude that has been the root of our suffering, we eliminate the cause of our own suffering as well as the suffering of others. Lama Zopa writes, "even if a person does not know what virtue is and how to accumulate it or what non-virtue is and how to avoid it, if he has less selfishness, he automatically has more good heart."[2]

This Buddhist understanding is not dissimilar to Jesus' teaching that by losing our life for his sake, we gain life, but those who seek to save their lives will lose them. That means that Christians seek to develop the same mind-set Buddhists aim to develop in this meditation. For both Christians and Buddhists, focusing on the other rather than on the self is life-giving.

The exercise of exchanging the self with others is designed to encourage us to put greater focus on the needs and desires of others, to develop a commitment to cherish others and wish them to have all that is good and excellent. It is based on a simple logic: that the self is only one and others are (from a Buddhist standpoint) limitless. By any rational way of thinking, the countless others become more important than the single self. When I engage in this meditation, I always think of a line in one of the *Star Trek* movies, where Mr. Spock says to Captain Kirk, "The needs of the many outweigh the needs of the few, or the one." The goal is to internalize at a deep level this exchange of the self with others.

To be very clear, the goal is not to feel that our own needs and desires have no importance at all. This is an important warning for two reasons. First, some people become so dedicated to caring for others that they do not realize their own legitimate needs are being neglected. That can lead to relationships of codependency that are healthy for neither the person who is neglecting her own needs nor the person for whose sake her needs are being neglected. Jesus was not a codependent and does not want that for us either. Loving like Jesus does not mean sacrificing our health and well-being to take care of others. We cannot work on behalf of others if we don't also take care of our own needs.

Second, from a Christian standpoint, desire has a role. Our authentic desires are a way we hear God's voice and thus are important motivators for our actions on behalf of God. We need to be attentive not to become so wholly absorbed in the needs of others that we fail to pay attention to our own desires. The goal is simply to recognize that our natural way of seeing ourselves as being of paramount importance is harmful and misguided.

What I present here does not reflect major changes from the way I practiced this meditation as a Tibetan Buddhist—the logic that is the basis of the meditation is not linked to any particular system of religious thought. The changes I made were designed simply to root the practice within the Christian tradition. These changes include introduction of the Christian understanding that all of us are equal in having been created in the image and likeness of God and the idea of putting on the mind of Christ, the supreme example for Christians of exchanging self for others. At the end, I add the familiar Ignatian colloquy. The central part of the meditation, however, is largely the same as a Buddhist would engage in it, with the exception that I refer to the large human population of the world rather than to infinite sentient beings; because Buddhists believe in multiple realms of existence and see all beings in all of those realms as well as humans as objects of our concern, the Buddhist meditation uses language of "infinite" beings.

Some might approach this practice with skepticism. If you just sit down and read the meditation, you can easily agree at an intellectual level, "Yeah, sure, countless is more important than one," but that intellectual assent will have no deep or lasting (or perhaps even temporary) effect on your behavior. This meditation is a good example of the importance of combining analytic meditation and stabilization meditation, as I discussed in the introduction to Part III. The goal is to "see" this reality at a much deeper level, which can be done only by engaging in the exercise in a concentrated way. That is the reason why, several times during the meditation, you should call back to your mind the image of yourself on one side and countless other people on the other, to develop a felt sense of the error of the self-cherishing heart. As soon as you feel some real softening of the self-cherishing heart, you should rest in that feeling and realization. If you practice this over and over again, it will begin to have a real effect on how you behave and how you view the relative importance of yourself and others.

Chapter 9

The Four Immeasurables

As when her one beloved son is sick a mother will think about him more, over and over, and her compassion will thus increase, by reciting the prayer of the four immeasurables and doing the meditation many times over, your loving kindness and compassion will increase.

Lama Thubten Zopa Rinpoche, *Lama Tsongkhapa Guru Yoga*

THE MEDITATION

Begin by contemplating the compassion Jesus felt for all the people with whom he came in contact, prayerfully reflecting on these lines:

He felt compassion for them because they were like sheep without a shepherd" (Mk 6:34).

When He went ashore, He saw a large crowd, and felt compassion for them and healed their sick. (Mt 14:14).

Stay with these lines, letting your mind form an image of Jesus caring for sick, feeling pity for all those in pain, until you experience a real sense of the compassion Jesus experienced toward all of the people he encountered during his ministry.

With Jesus by your side, consider how much people suffer because they are controlled by anger and attachment to things or

124

to other people. The strength of those delusions causes people to undergo great suffering and create the cause of suffering in the lives of others. Call to mind specific occasions when your own anger or attachment led you to do things that were not loving and that caused pain to others.

Now call to mind specific times when the anger or attachment of people you know or come in contact with has made them do things that were not loving and caused pain to you or to others.

Consider the ways in which anger and attachment underlie world conflicts and social problems. Call to mind some examples— the conflict between Arabs and Israelis, the anger that prompts terrorist attacks, the greed that incites companies to engage in financial improprieties that operate to the detriment of their shareholders and employees, or the greed that sanctions harmful exploitation of the environment.

After spending some time considering how much suffering results from anger and attachment, generate the thought of immeasurable equanimity, praying:

> *How wonderful it would be if everyone were able to abide in equanimity, free of bias, attachment, and anger. May they abide in this way. I shall help them to abide in this way. Lord Jesus, please guide and strengthen me to be able to do so.*

As you pray these words, take in the anger and attachment that causes the suffering of others. Visualize the anger and attachment coming toward you in the form of pollution, or as a deadly sharp weapon, or in the form of terrifying wild animals, whatever is most effective.

As the visualized pollution comes toward you, intentionally absorb it, allowing it to attack all of your thoughts and inclination to cherish the self. Allow the pollution to absorb and completely annihilate the self-cherishing impulse. When it does, allow the pollution to dissipate until it is completely gone. Let it become like water on hot sand; it evaporates as you approach it. When you reach the sand there is no longer a drop of water. When you feel some loosening of the self-cherishing self, stay with that sense.

If you find yourself resisting the pollution (or other image) as it comes toward you, focus on the source of the resistance. Ask yourself: what is keeping me from taking on the anger and attachment? Remembering that Jesus is by your side, ask him to give you the grace to overcome the obstacle. Feel that Jesus is taking in the suffering-causing anger and attachment along with you, making your task so much easier.

Next consider how gifted you are. Look at yourself and your life. Consider that you have a home with a comfortable bed to sleep in every night and food on the table. Look at your possessions. Your talents. Your friends. Your family. Your freedom to practice your religion. Your health. Take a long look at all of the things and qualities you have been gifted with.

Consider how many people lack those things that bring happiness to your life. People without family. Without friends. Without a talent they have identified to nurture.

Now generate the thought of immeasurable loving kindness, praying:

> *How wonderful it would be if everyone had happiness and its causes. May they have these. I shall help them to have these. Lord Jesus, please guide and strengthen me to be able to do so.*

As you pray these words, dedicate your body, your possessions, your merit—all you have—to everyone who needs the things you have been gifted with. With joy and generosity, send all of these things to them in the form of white light that emanates from your body. Let the light go out in all directions.

Watch what happens to the self-cherishing impulse as you do this. Allow the impulse to hold onto things for yourself dissipate as you send out all that you have to others. Again, when you feel some loosening of the self-cherishing self, stay with that sense.

If you find yourself feeling stingy, resisting the giving over of your gifts and self to others, put your attention on the source of that resistance. Feel where it is coming from. And, again recalling that Jesus is right by your side, consider all that he gave over out of love for us and ask him to help you to let go of your resistance.

Next consider all of the many ways in which people suffer— from war, illness, poverty, accidents. Given the state of the world today, it is easy to come up with examples. Allow some of the headlines you have read about conflicts, natural disasters, industrial accidents, and crime to flow through your mind, as though you were looking through a picture album. Really picture the suffering caused by attacks on the World Trade Center, the tsunami in Japan, earthquakes in China, the war in Iraq.

With Jesus, let your heart be filled with compassion for all of those who experience such suffering and generate the thought of immeasurable compassion, praying:

How wonderful it would be if everyone were free from suffering and its causes. May they be free. I shall help them to be free. Lord Jesus, please guide and strengthen me to be able to do so.

As you pray, let yourself feel your desire to help free others from suffering, allowing your feeling of love and compassion to well up inside of you.

Send your love and compassion for all people out in all directions in the form of white light emanating from your body.

If you feel any hesitation, allow a part of your mind to examine it as you continue to send your compassion out to the world. See if you can find the source of the hesitation and ask Jesus' help to let go of it. Again, when you feel any loosening of the self-cherishing thought, stay with that feeling.

Finally, acknowledge your desire that no one ever be separated from the ultimate happiness the comes from union with God, that they enjoy not just temporal happiness and relief from worldly suffering, but that they be one with God.

Consider how wonderful it would be if there were no suffering, if everyone realized that they can never be separated from God and that they are destined for perfect union with him.

Generate the thought of immeasurable joyfulness, praying:

How wonderful it would be if everyone were able to recognize that they can never be separated from God and that they continue on a path toward union with God. May they do so. I shall help them to do so. Lord Jesus, please guide and strengthen me to be able to do so.

As you visualize the entire human race standing in front of you, see the causes of their suffering in the form of black smoke, or a weapon, or wild animal, as before. Visualize the cause of all the world's suffering coming to you. As you take it in, see it dissolve any impulse in you toward self-cherishing, leaving only your desire to help free others from suffering.

Now go back and repeat the four prayers several times, adding your own words if you like. And then speak to Jesus whatever words you wish—addressing both your hesitations and your desires.

COMMENTARY

The "four immeasurables" in Tibetan Buddhism are equanimity—the desire for everyone to be freed from attachment and aversion; loving kindness—the desire for everyone to be happy; compassion—the desire for all beings to be freed from suffering; and joyfulness—the desire that all beings experience the ultimate happiness of freedom from the continuous cycle of birth and death that Buddhists believe characterizes our existence. They are called "immeasurable" because the goal is to generate these feelings toward an immeasurable number of sentient beings.

Immeasurable. In other words: all. Not some—not just your friends and family, but all—even the Saddam Husseins, Osama bin Ladens, Charles Mansons, and Timothy McVeighs of the world. A Christian has no difficulty saying the same thing—that the feelings expressed in the "four immeasurables" are ones we wish to generate toward everyone, although a Christian would frame the fourth in terms of union with God rather than escape from cyclic existence.

The instructions for the meditation are adapted from my notes on a commentary given by Lama Thubten Zopa Rinpoche. Lama Zopa's advice was to go through each of the four parts very slowly, thinking of specific people or situations. The more we can envision particular situations and people the more powerful the meditation becomes. Merely reciting the words without the accompanying mental activity is far less beneficial.

I adapted the verses of the prayer included in the meditation from the practice of Avalokiteshvara (Chenrezig in Tibetan), the Bodhisattva of Infinite Compassion. Tibetan Buddhists believe that Avalokiteshvara may appear anywhere to help any being in any kind of danger or distress. Each of the verses has four parts: a wish, an aspiration, a resolve, and a request for inspiration.

Lama Zopa's formulation of the prayer, the basis for the one I present, speaks in terms of our desires for the well-being of others. Geshe Rabten presents it differently, phrasing prayer of the first immeasurable, for example, as "how wonderful it would be if I and all sentient beings could abandon all attachment and aversion towards each other."[1] The focus is on our own suffering as well as the suffering of others. You may at times wish to try the alternative formulation.

I made a number of modifications to the prayer to make the meditation more appropriate for Christians. First, the original speaks of the person making the prayer as "causing" others' happiness and freedom from suffering. In recognition of the fact that we labor *with* God and do nothing by our own power, I changed "cause" to "help" and emphasized Jesus' presence with us during the meditation. Second, where the original prayer seeks inspiration from Chenrezig, I have changed it to a prayer to Jesus, seeking his guidance and strength, rather than merely his inspiration. Again, this is to emphasize that for Christians we do nothing on our own; we always work with God and with the grace of God. Finally, I changed the last prayer, which in the original refers to the Buddhist goal of rebirth in one of the upper realms and ultimately liberation, to speak of the Christian goal of union with God. This does not disturb the original idea of bringing to others a lasting happiness and peace rather than temporary happiness; it merely replaces the Buddhist understanding of what that means with a Christian one.

The other modification I made was to replace the language of emptiness with language of loosening of the self-cherishing self. Emptiness is a familiar concept for Buddhists. Christians don't tend to use that word in the same way. Lama Thubten Zopa Rinpoche's instruction at that point was to recognize, while breathing out white light, that the "I" that is meditating is "merely labeled on the aggregates," a typical Tibetan formulation. I substitute language of self-cherishing. I think Christians can identify with this more easily and ultimately it does nothing to distort the purpose or impact of the meditation.

This meditation uses a version of the tong-len meditation presented in chapter 6. The specifics are slightly different, but it employs the same general approach—taking in suffering and sending out compassion and love.

In the meditation I encourage you to focus on any fear or hesitation that arises. That such feelings arise is not bad—it is actually a good thing; it suggests that the meditation is having an effect. So when such feelings arise, don't try to push them away as unworthy, which is the natural tendency of many people. This is very important. We can't root out our fears unless we identify them and we can't identify them if we shove them aside when they arise. The goal is to observe the fears that arise without judgment to see if you can identify the source of the feeling. Then you can talk about the particulars of your fear and hesitation with Jesus.

You can do the entire meditation as I have presented it in one sitting. Alternatively, if you only have a short time available for prayer, or if you really want to focus on one of the qualities, spend an entire prayer period focused on only one of the four immeasurables. Geshe Rabten suggests praying the prayer every day, including it as a preliminary part of whatever other prayer practice we engage in.

Once you have gained some familiarity with the practice, you can use it at any time, just as you can the basic tong-len practice. If you are walking down the street or sitting in your office or home and see or experience something that calls to you for a response of equanimity, or joy, or loving kindness, or compassion, you can immediately do a short form of that portion of the meditation practice. St. Paul said, "Pray without ceasing" (1 Thes 5:17). This is a good example of a meditation that offers a means of doing exactly that. The same is also true of many of the other meditations I present here.

If you engage in a practice like this with some regularity, the thoughts carried in the four prayers start to arise spontaneously. So instead of thinking about how bored you are performing some unwanted task, the thought arises of how others will benefit from your doing the task. Instead of focusing on how tired you are, your mind goes to the way others are dependent on your help.

I am not suggesting that selfish thoughts or concern with your own suffering will no longer arise if you do this meditation. However, a regular practice will allow you to get past such feelings more effectively when they do arise. The practice brings you peace and also helps others—both those who are the direct beneficiaries of your more other-motivated behavior and those who will benefit by your example.

Chapter 10

Inexhaustible Love

Genuine compassion . . . springs from the clear recognition of the experience of suffering on the part of the object of compassion, and from the realization that this creature is worthy of compassion and affection. Any compassionate feeling that arises from these two realizations cannot be swayed—no matter how the object of compassion reacts against you.

His Holiness the Dalai Lama, *The Good Heart*

THE MEDITATION

Begin by recognizing that you are in the presence of God and asking God for the grace to develop love and compassion toward all people.

Visualize yourself in the center of a crowd that extends in all directions.

Your closest living relatives—parents, children, siblings—are to your immediate left and right. All of your other relatives and your friends are standing behind you.

Visualize in front of you the people you don't consider friends—those you dislike or who have hurt you or those you love.

Visualize around them others whom you know from your school, work, church, or community, acquaintances you consider to be neither friends nor "enemies."

Beyond them, extending in all directions, visualize all of the other people who inhabit this planet. There is no feeling of being crowded. No feeling of tension. Just you and all the people around you.

Consider the fact that all of these people—your family, your friends, your acquaintances, your enemies, and strangers—all of them want to be happy and avoid suffering, just as you do.

All of them—from the best to the worst—are all trying to do the best they can with their lives.

All of them—regardless of their relationship to you—are made in the image and likeness of God and are loved unconditionally and infinitely by God.

Look at God standing before you, and see God gazing on you. As St. Ignatius would say: Behold God beholding you. See the love with which God looks at you. Really allow yourself to experience God's loving gaze. See yourself as God sees you.

Hear God saying to you, "Before I formed you in the womb, I knew you" (Jer 1:5)… "I have loved you with an everlasting love" (Jer 31:3)… "I have called you by name and you are mine" (Is 43:1). Take the time to let yourself be completely submerged in God's love.

Now allow yourself to experience the loving gaze of those who hold you closest to them—a child or a parent or a best friend. See yourself as that person sees you.

As you look upon yourself with the same love with which God looks upon you and as those who hold you closest look upon you, generate a strong feeling of love in your heart. Think of someone you love very much (one of the same people looking upon you with so much love) and let your loving feeling for this person arise. Really let your warm, loving feeling for that person arise and allow it to completely suffuse your being.

As you feel the love arising, visualize it as a warm, bright light of energy filling and pulsating in your heart.

Imagine the warm, bright light of energy that is your love expanding from your heart and filling your entire body and mind.

Don't let it stop there—let love in the form of the warm, bright light of energy radiate out from your body to those around you. First let it flow out to your parents, your relatives, and your friends. Imagine the light radiating out from your body and touching each of them, filling them with your love.

As the warm, bright light of energy that is your love fills all of your friends and relatives, pray for their happiness and well-being. Generate the strong wish that they be free of all suffering—physical, emotional, mental, and spiritual—and that their lives be filled with love and peace.

Now focus on the people in front of you—those you dislike and those who have harmed you or hurt the ones you love. Realize that no matter how they have behaved toward you, they need your love as much as (or more than) your friends and relatives. Let the warm, bright light of energy that is your love radiate out from your heart to each one of them.

As you do this, pray for their happiness and well-being. Generate the strong wish that they be free of all of the anger and attachment that causes them to act badly toward you and others and that their lives be filled with love and peace.

Now let your love flow out even more widely in all directions so that the warm, bright light of energy extends out to everyone around you, all of the people you can see and those farther away that you can't even see. Open your heart completely and let your love flow with particular force to everyone who is suffering from any ailment of any kind—the lonely, the sick, the imprisoned, the homeless, the unemployed, the depressed. All those who are suffering.

As your love flows, pray for their happiness and well-being. Generate the strong wish that they be free of all suffering—physical, emotional, mental, and spiritual—and that their lives be filled with love and peace.

Pay attention to your feelings as you do this. If you find yourself worrying that your love will run out, remind yourself that love is unlimited and that you are a channel of God's inexhaustible love. A conduit of limitless spiritual energy. If you find yourself hesitating to extend your love to certain people, ask God's help to be able to send your love to them.

Concentrate for as long as possible on the feeling of love flowing out from you to all people.

As you bring your meditation to a close, realize that you have the potential to love everyone, even those who behave badly toward you or your loved ones, even those you don't know.

Ask for God's grace to overcome those things that make it difficult for you to love without distinction and without limit.

COMMENTARY

The Tibetan version of this meditation is often suggested as a complement to the *Friend, Enemy, Stranger* meditation adapted in chapter 5. You may wish to try it both as a stand-alone meditation and in conjunction with the other meditation.

Tibetan Buddhists recognize love as a natural quality of the mind. However, because our minds are under the sway of attachment and aversion, we offer our love selectively. The more we develop universal compassion, the less likely we are to fall under the sway of emotions like jealousy and anger. The goal is to develop the ability to live in a state of compassionate mind, not merely to try to will ourselves to act compassionately.

The idea of the meditation is to take our natural reserve of love—which we tap into most easily by accessing our love for those who are close to us—and to learn to extend that love to everyone, no matter what their relationship to us. That makes it a beautiful meditation for Christians, because the Buddhist thought here is similar to the Christian one; our Christian command is to love one another as Jesus loves us and to love our enemies, not just those who are good to us.

The meditation requires virtually no adaptation to make it accessible to Christians, except for the changes that naturally flow from the Christian recognition that our love originates in God and that we do all we do with the grace of God rather than on our own. Thus, I begin the meditation with the familiar request for the grace to develop love and compassion toward all people, and end it with the invitation to call upon God's help in overcoming those things that make it hard for us to love.

Early in the meditation I include an invitation to get in touch with God's love for you. This is an important step. Our ability to love others freely depends on seeing ourselves as loved. Many of us struggle with fully accepting God's incredible and unconditional love. I don't mean at the intellectual level; mouthing the words "God loves me unconditionally and infinitely" is easy. Rather, I mean knowledge to the core of your being. And so this step of this meditation is valuable in and of itself.

I reference St. Ignatius's instruction that we behold God beholding us. St. Ignatius suggests we begin all of our prayer periods by becoming aware of how God is gazing at us, by sitting in awareness of the eternally loving gaze of God. He suggests asking: Lord, what do you see when you look at me?

A poem by Daniel Ladinsky beautifully captures this sense of how God looks at us. It is called "Whenever He Looks at You." Ladinsky writes: "the delight a child can know tossing a ball into the air, my Lord confesses he experiences whenever he looks at you." That is what we are invited to believe.

Getting in touch with that sense of God's love is what ultimately will allow us to spread our love freely. Once we find ourselves immersed in the sea of God's love, we realize that there is nothing for us to do—nothing we can do—but be conduits of that love to the entire world. We realize that love is inexhaustible; we don't have to worry that it will run out. From a Christian perspective, this modification to the original meditation, while seemingly minor, is important. You want to experience a strong and deep sense of God's love for you—however long that takes—before following the remaining steps of the meditation.

You can even take this one portion of the meditation and make it the object of your prayer for an entire prayer period. That is particularly useful for those who are insecure about God's love for them. Many people have deep wounds that make it difficult to see themselves as lovable. They find it hard both to love themselves and to believe that others love them. They have difficulty believing in God's love for them as well. For such individuals, it is far more beneficial to spend extra time developing a felt sense of God's love than to immediately try to send love out to others. Working with a spiritual director or other guide is particularly useful for such people as well.

Two other suggestions of a practical nature: First, when visualizing the people around you, be as specific as possible. Don't just imagine a sea of unidentifiable "relatives and friends," "people I have difficulty with," and "acquaintances." Try to see the faces of real people in your life for all three categories. This will make the meditation more concrete and powerful.

Second, the instructions begin by asking you to visualize yourself in a crowd of people extending in all directions. I am a bit claustrophobic and sometimes when I hear that instruction, my reaction is to tense up as I start to visualize people pressing so close to me in all directions that I cannot breathe. I find it helpful to make a conscious effort to picture the crowd at least a couple of feet away from me so that I have plenty of breathing space. So visualize the crowd in a way that is comfortable to you, that allows you to proceed in a relaxed way without feeling crowded and tense.

There is no magic here. It is not a quick or easy process to move from our selective love to a love that embraces everyone. But if we sincerely engage in practices like this one, we can get more deeply in touch with our natural love—with our "God-love," which is offered freely to all and limitlessly to all. Again, as I have noted elsewhere, that does not mean we don't take care of ourselves, but rather that we withhold our love from no one.

Chapter 11

Giving the Four Elements

Just like space
And the great elements such as earth,
May I always support the life of all the boundless creatures.

Santideva, *A Guide to the Bodhisattva's Way of Life*

THE MEDITATION

Begin by recalling that you are in the presence of God and asking God for the grace to follow Jesus' example of boundless love and compassion.

Now reflect on Jesus' words in John's Gospel: "unless a grain of wheat falls into the earth and dies, it remains alone; but if it dies, it bears much fruit" (Jn 12:24).

Consider how Jesus gave up everything for us, including his physical life, and that he continues to nourish us with his body and blood.

Now reflect on Jesus' next words to his disciples: "He who loves his life loses it.... If anyone serves me, he must follow me; and where I am, there my servant will be also" (Jn 12:25–26).

Visualize Jesus standing before you, inviting you to do as he did—to give up all for the sake of others. Hear him say that he asks nothing of you that he has not already given and hear his assurance that whatever you give, he will be present, giving along with you. Throughout the meditation, try to retain an awareness of Jesus' presence and quiet encouragement.

Generate the desire to accept Jesus' invitation to follow his example, to do everything possible to alleviate others' suffering and provide for their needs, even if it comes at a great personal cost, perhaps even the cost of your own life. See Jesus beside you as you try to sincerely generate this desire.

Visualize yourself—your body and your entire being. With the desire to alleviate the suffering of others, allow your flesh and bones to be absorbed into the earth, to become one with the earth, creating mountains of earth for the comfort of others. Feel them doing so.

Watch the material of the mountains—made with your flesh and bones—become houses, roads, fields, and all of the various things that support the life and well-being of others. Visualize as extensively as possible, seeing all of the ways others use the material you have become.

Next, allow your blood and the other liquid parts of your body to be transformed into water, becoming lakes, streams, and rain. Watch the bodies of water swell and flow with the water created by your blood and the other liquids in your body.

Allow yourself to visualize all of the ways others enjoy the benefits of that water. See people with enough clean water to drink. Watch forests becoming lush and beautiful. Hear the rain falling to the earth to water crops. Again, visualize as extensively as possible, seeing all of the ways others enjoy the water you have provided.

At every stage of the meditation watch for any hesitation that arises. As you continue, allow part of your mind to examine the hesitation, to see where it comes from, becoming aware of what grace you need from Jesus to overcome it.

Now allow your breath to be absorbed into the wind and become oxygen for the survival of others. Watch the air around you cleansed and oxygenated by your breath. Visualize all of the people breathing in the air they need to live, clean, fresh air that has been created and nourished by your breath. See them gain in strength through your life-giving energy.

Next, allow the very life-giving heat of your body to become fire. Not a raging forest fire, but domestic fire that can be controlled and used. Contemplate all of the ways this benefits others—fire to cook with, heat to keep warm. See so many people benefiting from the life-giving heat you have offered them.

Finally, allow your two eyes to be absorbed into the sun and moon and in that way bring happiness and comfort to others, giving them light and the warmth they need to live.

Dedicate your flesh, your blood, your breath, your heat, your eyes—your entire physical being—to the support of others. As you contemplate all the people who benefit from your total self-offering, slowly pray

> *May I be the doctor and the medicine*
> *And may I be the nurse*
> *For all sick beings in the world*
> *Until everyone is healed....*

> *May I become an inexhaustible treasure*
> *For those who are poor and destitute;*
> *May I turn into all things they could need*
> *And may these be placed close beside them....*

> *May I be a protector for those without one,*
> *A guide for all travelers on the way;*

May I be a bridge, a boat, and a ship
For all who wish to cross.

May I be an island for those who seek one
And a lamp for those desiring light.[1]

Sit quietly for a time after completing the prayer, reflecting on your offering of self. Then, before ending your prayer time, spend some time in colloquy with Jesus. Talk about any difficulties you experienced. Ask for his help in becoming able to offer yourself as completely as he did.

COMMENTARY

This meditation is drawn from a teaching given by Lama Thubten Zopa Rinpoche on *Giving the Four Elements to Sentient Beings*. The prayer with which I end the meditation is not part of Lama Zopa's original instructions, but comes from Santideva's *A Guide to the Bodhisattva's Way of Life*.

At first blush this meditation may seem to be a greater stretch for a Christian than some of the others in this book. It seems very foreign to the type of prayer we usually engage in and the visualizations may seem strange (initially, even off-putting to some).

However, the more I reflected on it, the more fitting the meditation seemed to me for the faith that views Christ and his self-sacrifice—the giving over of his body and blood—as models for discipleship. At the Last Supper Jesus offered his body and blood as our food and drink. By his death, Jesus showed his willingness to give us everything, holding nothing back.

I open the prayer with Jesus' words to his disciples in St. John's Gospel. The words both foretell his death and explain why it had to occur: a grain of wheat must fall to the ground and die so that it may bring fruit. Thus was it necessary for the Son of Man to lay down his life for us.

Jesus makes absolutely clear, however, that these words do not apply only to him. Immediately after the parable of the grain of wheat, he goes on to say that anyone wishing to serve him must follow his example. Likewise, immediately after washing the feet of the disciples, Jesus says: "For I gave you an example that you also should do as I did to you" (Jn 13:15). And, of course, as Jesus offers his body and blood as food and drink to his disciples, he says, "do this in remembrance of me" (Lk 22:19).

Jesus is our model; our aim is to be as Christ to others. As I reflected on our call to be the body and blood of Christ to each other, the meditation's powerful imagery of giving our body and blood for the benefit of others no longer seemed so strange. What first appeared so foreign is in fact a very Eucharistic meditation, in which Christians should be able to engage if we take Jesus' teachings seriously.

I made several adaptations to the meditation. I started with the obvious one of beginning the prayer session by calling to mind Christ's teaching in John and his model of self-sacrifice, as a means of generating the desire to be as Christlike as possible. One should take enough time with those words to fully appreciate what Jesus was saying to his disciples—that he was talking about himself and about them, and to appreciate that he meant what he said.

Doing this meditation seriously will give rise to some hesitation and resistance. If it doesn't, it is a safe bet you are not doing it with enough concentration and openness; giving oneself over completely is not easy. Thus, in my version of the meditation I invite you to be conscious of Jesus' presence and support and to examine with him any hesitation that arises. The invitation is to allow a piece of the mind to be attentive to any hesitation that arises, to, spylike, investigate it to see from where it stems. Through this process of self-examination what will likely seem at first an amorphous, generalized fear may resolve into something more particular and defined that you can bring to prayer. I can't emphasize enough the importance of spending time with the hesitations and points of resistance that arise in our prayer. These are blockages that represent places where we need to do work with God.

Finally, the original meditation ended with a focus on emptiness. In Lama Zopa Rinpoche's instructions, at the point when you have no body left, only the mind, you should meditate on the lack of self-existent "I." Wanting to keep the focus on the aspect of total self-giving, I excluded that part of the instruction. I end the prayer instead with a passage from Santideva's text, the imagery of which I find beautiful. The prayer itself is worth spending some time with and I encourage a slow reading of it, really allowing the desires expressed in it to arise in you.

For some people, this will seem a strange exercise, notwithstanding its Eucharistic overtones. After all, we cannot literally dissolve our bodies or our bodily liquids, and the idea of our eyes becoming sun and moon will strike some as sounding like a fantastic children's story. But although none of these things is actually happening, the imagery is a tool, a way of developing seriousness of purpose in trying to engage in the total self-offering modeled by Jesus.

This is the last of the meditations I present that focuses in one way or another on developing universal love and compassion and replacing the self-cherishing heart with a heart that cherishes others. So let me close by addressing a misgiving that may be lurking in the minds of some. These meditations presuppose that you are committed to follow Jesus' command to love everyone, including those who are not good to you, and that you give with no expectation of reward. However, in a world in which it seems that so many want only to take without giving, even committed Christians are vulnerable to weariness and the fear of being taken advantage of. This is why, in this meditation and in others, I so frequently recommend that you talk to Jesus about the source of any hesitations that you feel and let Jesus speak to you on those issues. For all but the most spiritually developed among us, these hesitations and fears will arise and there is no value in pretending otherwise. But with God's grace we can become more like Christ— more giving, more loving, and more willing to give and love even when we do not receive love in return. We can, with God's grace, become the persons God wants us to be.

Chapter 12

Appreciating the Gifts of Our Birth

When we have meditated deeply on how valuable, rare, and fragile our human form is, the thought should arise in our mind that worldly, samsaric activities have as little essence as a husk of grain.

Lama Yeshe and Lama Zopa Rinpoche, *Wisdom Energy*

THE MEDITATION

Begin by asking for the grace to develop a deep appreciation for the life you have been given and the resolve to use it wisely.

Consider the many ways in which you have been blessed, the ways in which you have been given a life that allows you to respond to Christ's invitation to discipleship:

Contemplate first the richness of being born in a country in which you have access to the teachings of Christ and the means to develop your spiritual life. Consider what it would be like to live in a country without religious freedom, where you were unable to gather in communal worship, where Christians are attacked or abused because of their faith (as they still are in parts of our world today).

Imagine what it would be like not to be able to go to church or receive the Eucharist because you lived under a repressive or lawless regime.

Imagine what it would be like to be in a place where there were no spiritual teachers or mentors or spiritual friends, no one to guide you or walk with you on the spiritual path.

Consider that even if you lived in a place with religious freedom and spiritual teachers, you could have been born into a situation in which you had to expend so much energy just to survive that you had no time to devote to spiritual practice, perhaps working two or three jobs, or in a place where you had to spend a significant portion of each day gathering food and water. What would it have been like if you had been born without the leisure time for prayer and meditation?

Next consider that you could have been born with a mind completely antagonistic or indifferent toward the Word of God. What would it be like to have been born without interest, desire, or devotion to the Word?

Or you could have been born with a severe handicap or limitation that prevented you from understanding the Word and being able to act on it.

Consider all the ways in which your life could have been different, all of the conditions into which you could have been born that would have made it much more difficult, if not impossible, for you to follow a path of Christian discipleship. Be as concrete as you can in thinking of examples of the many ways your life could have been different in a way that would have hindered your ability to grow in Christ.

Realize how fortunate you are to have been blessed with the ability to hear Christ's teachings and act on them.

Now realize how many people do not have the benefits that you do, who were not born into so fortunate a situation. Spend some time considering the many different states of life into which people are born, appreciating how fortunate your situation is compared with theirs. Again, be as concrete as you can, really examining the difficult circumstances in which so many people find themselves, and which make life so much harder for them than it is for you.

Generate *joy* that you have been gifted with a life that affords you the opportunity to grow in discipleship and become Christ in the world.

Generate *gratitude* that you have been so gifted.

Generate the *resolve* to use the life you have been given wisely.

As you bring your reflection to a close, speak to God whatever words are in your heart: express your gratitude for the gifts you have been given and ask for the grace to use your life more fully to further God's plan.

COMMENTARY

One of the first teachings and meditations of the *Lam-Rim* is sometimes referred to as meditating on our "perfect human rebirth." This is a basic Tibetan idea on which oral teachings are frequently given. Even when presenting teachings on other subjects, Tibetan teachers will often begin by talking about the perfect human rebirth.

The idea of the meditation is to appreciate the "perfect" human life you have been given—to understand its rarity and develop the conviction that you must use it to the fullest extent. In the words of the great teacher Lama Je Tsongkhapa:

> The perfect human form, more precious than jewels,
> Is only to be gained at this present time.
> It is most difficult to find yet easily decays,
> Passing light a lightning flash in the sky.

> Thinking that such is the nature of life,
> It is necessary to take its essence
> Throughout the day and the night.
> I, the yogi, have practiced like this.
> You who desire liberation please
> Train yourself in the very same way. [1]

Tibetan Buddhists believe that true happiness comes only from Dharma practice. The idea of the meditation is to gain a deep intuitive knowledge of the value of your perfect human rebirth in order to recognize the importance of not wasting it: to develop an appreciation of how difficult and rare it is to have all of the preconditions necessary to be able to engage in spiritual practice. In trying to convey the preciousness of the perfect human rebirth, one lama from whom I took teachings offered an analogy to a lake in which jewels naturally occur. To come to such a place and fail to gather up as many jewels as we could carry, he observed, would be an incredible wasted opportunity. His language brings to mind Jesus' parables of the buried treasure and pearl of great price (Mt 13:44–47), in which a man who finds treasure in a field sells all he has to buy the field and the merchant who finds a pearl of great value sells everything he has to obtain the pearl.

The Buddhist hope is that by meditating deeply on the value and fragility of this perfect human rebirth, we will see everything other than spiritual practice as having "as little essence as a husk of grain." Tibetan lamas tell their students that whenever they face difficulties in their practice they should meditate on this perfect human rebirth and the precious opportunity it offers. Some teachers recommend doing the meditation every day. In the words of Lama Yeshe and Lama Thubten Zopa Rinpoche, "the more we meditate on these matters by looking into our own life and those of our acquaintances, the more we shall realize [the need to] make a sincere effort to tame our mind."[2]

Christians have a broader view of what is a valuable use of our human lives. For us, lives of Christian discipleship include both prayer and activities to model Christ in the world. Nonetheless, Christians are no less likely than Buddhists to fail to appreciate the value of the life they have been given. And they are no less likely to let other things distract them from prayer (as well as from living the life Christ encourages us to live). Many of us find it easy to say we don't have time for prayer, or for retreat, or for other spiritual exercises. We have heard the Word, we have a level of commitment to Jesus and to discipleship, but we find it easy to put off serious engagement with our faith and our spiritual growth. We can, at times, be like the seed that fell among thorns in the parable of the sower, "the man who hears the word, and the worry of the world and the deceitfulness of wealth choke the word, and it becomes unfruitful" (Mt 13:7, 22). This meditation is a useful one to combat the feeling that we have no time to pray and to help us develop a greater commitment to our spiritual growth.

In addition to serving as a spur to spiritual practice, Tibetans teach this meditation as an antidote or opponent force to depression and other negative feelings. It has the same value for Christians. Many of the problems we experience stem from the way we feel about our lives—our failure to appreciate how good our situation really is. The meditation helps focus, not on those things we lack—which is where the mind so easily goes—but all the good we have in our lives. It helps us to rejoice in what we have, rather than bemoan what we lack.

A few comments about my adaptation: First, I do not employ the term "perfect" to describe the life we have been given, as the Tibetan form of the meditation does. None of our lives are perfect.

Moreover, many of us have a problem with perfectionism, which creates the danger that the term will be a distraction. I have some reservations about dispensing with the term, however, because it does help convey the preciousness of what we have been given. We have been given gifts of inestimable value.

Second, because my adaptation is addressed to Christians, I refer to birth rather than rebirth. Tibetan Buddhists believe people can be reborn into any one of six different realms, and they begin the meditation by contemplating the other realms into which they could be reborn, examining how difficult it would be to meditate and to overcome delusions in those realms. They consider their freedom from having been reborn in one of the three lower realms where there is no freedom to practice Dharma because of unimaginable suffering and deep ignorance, and they spend time contemplating what life is like in each of those three realms. Thus, for example, Buddhists would reflect on the fact that as humans we have minds capable of understanding cause and effect, capable of understanding the causes of suffering and the path to the elimination of suffering, but if we had been born as animals, no such understanding would be possible. Buddhists would go on to consider their freedom from rebirth in the god realms, where practice is impossible because of the continual distraction of objects of the senses, where life is too pleasurable to have any motivation to attain enlightenment. Contemplation of the existence of less fortunate other lives also functions as a motivational tool in a different way; part of the motivation for using the perfect human rebirth well is to avoid rebirth in one of the nonhuman realms.

Because Christians do not share the Buddhist belief in reincarnation, my focus is on this human life, hence my change from "perfect human rebirth" to appreciating the gifts of our birth. I also focus on religious freedom and awareness of Christ, whereas the original meditation speaks of being born in a land where Buddha's teachings are available.

The most important thing in doing the meditation is to be really concrete. In order to generate a deep appreciation of this life and the resolve to use it well, you want to put yourself in the situations you visualize as though you were really there. Really get a sense of how difficult it would be to practice your faith under certain conditions and compare that with your present situation. It also helps to get a sense of how easily you could lose the beneficial situation you have.

Near the end of the meditation I spoke of three feelings you are seeking to generate: joy, gratitude, and resolve. The goal is to generate joy that you have been gifted with a life that affords the opportunity to transform your mind and grow in Christian discipleship. Gratitude to God for this gift, recognizing that many people lack what we have. And the resolve to use the gift we have been given well, not to squander this precious life we have been given.

As I mentioned, some Tibetan teachers advise their students to meditate on the perfect human rebirth every day, to help them develop a strong and positive motivation for practice. Even if you don't want to follow this advice, a short exercise in gratitude is a wonderful way to begin each day. You could easily construct a short version of the practice that allows you to daily generate a sense of gratitude for the ways in which your life is blessed and affords you the opportunity to grow in your relationship to God. As one of my students said to me after doing this meditation, "Gratitude is so important. Even on my worst day, I can always find gratitude for the smallest thing if I try."

Chapter 13

Impermanence

Our dependence on impermanent things and clinging to the rainbow-like happiness they bring cause only disappointment and grief, not satisfaction and contentment.

Sangye Khadro (Kathleen McDonald), *How to Meditate*

THE MEDITATION

Begin by asking God for the grace to gain a deep appreciation of the impermanence of the things of this world.

Mindfully observe your breathing. As you inhale, notice the trunk of your body expanding as the air you take in fills your chest and abdominal area. Feel the changes in your rib cage and in other parts of your body as you take in air. Do the same as you exhale, noticing your abdomen and chest fall as the air leaves your body. Continue doing this for some time, noticing any and all changes in your body as you inhale and exhale.

Now starting at the top of your head, slowly become aware of your body. Start by putting your focus on the top of your head, noticing the feelings there.

Slowly let your awareness move down your head, placing your awareness firmly, first, on your eyes...then your ears...then your nose...then your mouth. Examine each in turn, noticing the feelings there, noticing especially how the sensations change.

Do the same with each part of your body, from your head down to your toes. Take your time doing this.

Make sure not to limit your awareness to the outside of your body; spend time being aware of your internal organs, your blood, your bones, your muscles, and nerves.

Examine each part. Be aware of its shape...its size...its texture...its feel.

After you've examined each individual part of the body, continue to be aware of your body as a whole, of how the various parts work together to sustain your life—the nerves carrying impulses to and from your brain...the veins and arteries carrying blood to and from your heart...the beating of your heart.

Focus your attention on the smallest parts that make up your body. You can't see them or feel them, but consider the fact that your entire body is composed of cells that are constantly in motion and constantly reproducing themselves—old cells die and new ones replace them.

When you get a strong feeling of the impermanence of any part of the body, stay with that feeling for as long as it lasts or as long as you can keep your attention focused on it. When it fades, go to another part of your body.

Now focus your awareness on your mind and all of its parts—your thoughts, your feelings, your perceptions. Watch as your mind focuses on first one thing and then another. An itch on your nose...a sensation of heat or cold...something you hear...a thought. Don't try to change or affect anything. Simply be aware of the flow of experiences of your consciousness. Watch the object of your attention change moment by moment without any interference or effort on your part.

When you get a strong feeling of the impermanence of any part of the mind, stay with that feeling for as long as it lasts or as long as you can keep your attention focused on it. When it fades, go to another part of your mind.

After you have focused on the parts of the body and mind for some period of time, slowly shift your attention outside of your body to the world around you. Start by being aware of your immediate surroundings, starting with the chair or cushion you are sitting on...then moving on to the physical look of the room you are in—its shape, its furnishings, and so on...then the temperature and feel of the room.

Contemplate the fact that each of these is constantly changing. Some things are easily apparent—the temperature of the room, for example. But other changes are more subtle: even the furniture, which appears to be solid and static, is actually composed of bundles of energy, tiny particles that are constantly changing.

Try to develop a feeling of the impermanent nature of even the most solid-seeming things around you. Again, any time you get a strong sense of impermanence, stay with the feeling until it fades or as long as you can keep your attention focused on it.

After some time, move your attention to the physical area outside of the room—the rest of the building, the garden and street outside, the cars on the street. Keep expanding your awareness outward to take in all of the surrounding areas.

Contemplate the fact that everything in your range of experience and beyond is changing subtly, moment by moment. Some changes are obvious, like the trees that keep losing their leaves and growing new ones. Or the character of the light from the sun as the day progresses.

Other changes are more subtle. You can't see the rocks eroding, but you know it is happening. You can't see any change in the bark of the trees, but you know that insects, birds, and the weather are causing the bark to transform. Nothing remains the same from one moment to another. Again, stay with this until you can develop a feeling of the impermanent nature of even the most solid things in the external world.

When you experience a strong feeling of the impermanent, constantly changing nature of things, keep your attention on that feeling for as long as you can. When the feeling starts to fade, move to another object of awareness.

As you bring your meditation to a close, spend a few minutes reflecting on how it helps you to have experienced a sense of the impermanence of all of the things of the world and give thanks to God for allowing you to have that experience.

COMMENTARY

This can be a difficult meditation. The object of meditation and the awareness called for are much more subtle than in the other meditations I present. While parts of the meditation concern objects that are easy for us to focus on and whose impermanence is easy for us to "see," imagination is required for consideration of the cells that make up our body or the moment-by-moment change in something with the apparent solidity of a chair. People often have difficulty the first time they do the meditation. So it is important to understand that the meditation addresses a fundamental delusion in how we see the world and ourselves.

Impermanence—the idea that nothing is permanent and everything changes moment by moment—is one of the fundamental truths of Buddhism. The transience of the world is also part of Christian thought. Indeed, change is a fundamental reality of human existence, not merely a doctrine or truth of any one faith tradition. Having said that, the Buddhist and Christian concepts are different in a very important respect— for Buddhists there is nothing that has any permanent existence, whereas Christians would say that everything passes away except for God.

Buddhist or Christian, we are habituated not to see impermanence. We notice the obvious changes—children get older, leaves fall from the trees, roads suffer wear and tear, our clothes get too small for us. For the most part, however, we experience the world as permanent and we cling to people and things as though they were permanent. This is especially true of our sense of ourselves: we cling to a view of the self as having solidity. Think about how easily you come to view the adjectives with which you describe yourself as unchanging parts of your person. We say, "I am a shy person" or "I am a happy person" and believe that these aspects of our personality define who we now are and always will be.

The result of clinging to persons and things as permanent is frustration and unhappiness. Our expectation that things are permanent is thwarted time and again. We are disappointed when we cannot hold onto things as they were (or as we thought they were). This is not a new revelation: we all have some recognition of the fact that human beings are, on the whole, very uncomfortable with change.

Thus, it is important to develop the recognition that things are in a constant state of flux, to accept the fundamental truth that impermanence is the state of all things. Of course, as with so many fundamental truths, the words are easy. We can say everything is impermanent and have some understanding of what that means at an intellectual level. But that is not how we experience the world. Instead, we experience things as permanent and cling to them.

For both Buddhists and Christians, then, it is important to gain a deep experiential realization of impermanence. There are a number of prayer and meditation practices in the Buddhist tradition that help us to gain that experiential understanding, help us accept the changing nature of things. One is vipassana meditation, which comes out of the Theravadan tradition of Buddhism, and for which I provide some basic instruction in chapter 20. Another is this Tibetan Buddhist analytical meditation. The aim in both cases is to help us learn to cling less tenaciously to an illusory state and be more accepting of things as they are.

The meditation I present here is virtually identical to the meditation as I learned it. Except for opening and closing with an awareness of the presence of God, no adaptation was necessary.

As I have said, this meditation is more difficult than most of the others I present in this book because many of the objects of focus are so subtle. So with this one even more than the others, try to reserve judgment until you have tried the practice a few times.

Chapter 14

Death

Mindfulness of impermanence and death is important at the beginning of the day, to impel one to engage in the practice; it is important in the middle, to maintain one's energy; and it is important at the end, to induce one to complete the practice.

Geshe Rabten, *The Essential Nectar*

THE MEDITATION

Begin by recognizing that you are in the presence of God and asking God for the grace to gain a deep appreciation of the uncertainty of when death will come.

Consider the fact that death is certain. Death is inevitable; no human being has ever avoided it. Picture in your mind, one by one, the people you know who have died, starting with your family members, then acquaintances, then people you have heard of who have died, then historical figures. In your mind, list name after name to deepen your sense of the reality of the universality of death.

Next consider that your own life is inexorably diminishing. Reflect on the words of Lama Yeshe,

> From the first instant of life impermanence is with us. From the moment of conception decay begins. In the second moment of life a change has already occurred and the first moment has disappeared. That is impermanence and death.[1]

Visualize your life as a lighted candle, steadily burning down. Each breath you take brings you closer to death. Each hour that passes is one fewer hour of life. Each day that passes brings your death one day closer. As you consider the passing days, watch the candle get smaller and smaller.

After spending some time considering the certainty of death, realize that while death is certain, it is not certain when you will die. Our life span is unknown to us. Some people wake up in the morning and are dead by that afternoon. Some go to bed, having set their alarm clock and expecting to rise the next morning, and die in their sleep. Some people live to be ninety-four, others die at birth or in childhood. Often, there is no warning at all that the time of death has arrived.

Yet consider how much time we spend plotting out our future. We plan next summer's vacation. We wonder about our next job. We plan a menu for next week's dinner party. We worry about whether we've saved enough for our retirement years. Consider all the plans you have made, all conceived with the assumption that these things will definitely occur—or at least that you will be around to see whether they occur or not.

We make all sorts of plans with the expectation that our lives will go on into the future, yet any and all of those plans could become irrelevant at any moment. We could die in the middle of breakfast... while writing a letter... while driving to work... while sitting in a movie theater. We can die with no warning at all, with no time to "put our affairs in order."

As you consider the uncertainty of the time of death, realize that there are many causes of death. Accidents. Illness. Violence. Any of these may strike at any time. Our bodies are so fragile in so many ways; anything can cause our death.

We know we will die, but we don't know when. Let that reality sink in.

Now ask yourself: what will help you at the moment of your death?

Friends and relatives? Ask yourself: Will they be able to prevent death from coming? Will the fact that you have lots of friends and family, or that you are popular with many people, do anything to slow the coming of death?

Possessions and riches? We know you can't take it with you, but can you use it to bribe death? Will anything you have—all the money in the bank, the house, the car, the jewelry—will any of it make a difference at the moment of your death?

The beauty or strength of your body? Will it make a difference how beautiful you are? Will your strength enable you to prevent death from coming?

Skills and talents? Will it matter that you were a great pianist or athlete or writer? Will any of your accomplishments allow you to cheat death?

Go through every worldly person, possession, and characteristic, everything you can think of until you are convinced that there is nothing of this physical world that can help you at the moment of your death. This life will become nothing. We will be separated from our friends. Our wealth and possessions and accomplishments must be left behind. Everything, absolutely everything, must eventually be left behind.

There is only one source of help at death: God. What we do in this life to grow spiritually, to grow in discipleship and deepen our relationship with God is the only thing that will enable us to face death with joy and confidence, knowing that physical death is a doorway into a deeper and permanent union with God.

Now consider how easy it is during your lifetime to get caught up in meaningless pursuits. How easy it is to fill our lives with things that distract us from our discipleship. How hard we find it to make time for prayer and other spiritual practice. How much we avoid any serious effort to discern our role in God's plan for salvation. How often we forget that we even have a role in that plan.

Now generate a firm resolve to use the time you have in a meaningful fashion. To make time to deepen your relationship with God. To generate greater faith, hope, and love. To labor with God for as long as you have in this life.

COMMENTARY

One of the early meditations of the *Lam-Rim* is a meditation on death. From a Tibetan Buddhist perspective, the main obstacle to spiritual practice is attachment to the things of this world. "The Eight Worldly Concerns" (the subject of a later meditation) involve obtaining pleasures such as good food, praise, material gain, and good reputation, and avoiding their opposites.

We live under the illusion that our life will last a long time, an illusion that has consequences. When we imagine that we have a long life ahead of us, it is easy to focus only on obtaining happiness and avoiding the sufferings of this life. Lama Thubten Zopa Rinpoche explained, "We have the hallucination that this life will last a long time, that having a human body, friends, comforts, enjoyments will last. By trusting the appearance that life will last a long time, the complete hallucination, we spend this life in anger and attachment. We regard happiness of this life as most important. With that mind, nothing gets done."[2] Even though we know we will die, for most of us that ending seems so far off. And so we always believe there will be enough time to prepare later. We live with a false security, forgetting (to use a phrase I heard from the Dalai Lama) that death is like a lord who strikes at will.

For Buddhists, meditating on death is intended to counter our obsession with the Eight Worldly Concerns by overcoming the illusion that there will always be more time. The purpose is not to make anyone depressed, but to generate enthusiasm to practice. If we truly realize that any moment could be our last we would behave differently than we do. Geshe Rabten draws this analogy: "If, while a man, led by soldiers, is walking the last mile to his place of execution, people offer him all sorts of things such as flowers and good bread which normally make one happy, it will not cheer him up in the least, since he will be completely absorbed in the thought of his coming death."[3]

The alternative is to die with fear and remorse. Lama Zopa Rinpoche put it like this:

One is expecting to live long, but one day suddenly the exhalation is strong and inhalation is weak. Then, even if one recognizes "I am dying," there is no time to do any preparation for the happiness of future lives; it is too late. Suddenly the bright appearance of this life stops. Then, at this time, no matter how many friends and relatives are surrounding you, there is nothing they can do except stand around with fear and worry, their eyes filled with tears, looking at your body, the dead body. Even if doctors are called, no matter how many, there is nothing they can do. At that time, no matter how upset you feel, there is nothing you can do; no matter how scared you are, nothing you can do. You cannot ask the Lord of Death to wait. And at that time, whatever work isn't finished is ended by impermanence and death; one is unable to finish studying—ended by impermanence and death; writing books—so busy writing books—unable to finish— ended by impermanence and death. Another started eating— before finished—death happened. One started to write a letter—before signing, death happened. One plans to take ordination, before the chance, death happened. One began traveling and before reaching home, unable to reach home— death happened. Plane crash, car crash. So it is extremely important to live your life so that when death occurs you are happy—it is like going on a picnic or going home.[4]

I find Lama Zopa's language here particularly powerful, and one alternative for prayer would be to simply read this passage slowly and prayerfully, contemplating the images he presents.

Death is not the same for Christians as it is for Buddhists. For a Buddhist, unless enlightenment is achieved in this lifetime, death means rebirth, possibly into a realm below the human one. For Christians, what follows death is resurrection and complete union with God, although many Christians believe in purgatory as a way station between earth and heaven. Christ's resurrection is a victory over death for all of us.

Nonetheless, Christian tradition understands the value of an awareness of death and the need to use our lives meaningfully. In the parable of the "rich fool" in Luke's Gospel, Jesus holds up for ridicule the rich man who plans to tear down his barn and build bigger ones so that he can store his grains for many years. God's response: "You fool! This very night your soul is required of you; and now who will own what you have prepared?" (Lk 12:16–20). Later in the same chapter of Luke, Jesus tells another parable, the punch line of which is, "if the head of the house had known at what hour the thief was coming, he would not have allowed his house to be broken into. You too, be ready; for the Son of Man is coming at an hour that you do not expect" (Lk 12:39–40). Christian preachers try to convey the same message to their hearers, asking them to consider, for example, what they would do differently if they knew they had only three months left to live.

Talking to his disciples about what will happen in the "days of the Son of Man," Jesus reminds them that people were eating and drinking when the Flood came and destroyed them and people were selling and planting when Sodom was destroyed. And he says that "on that night there will be two in one bed; one will be taken and the other will be left. There will be two women grinding at the same place; one will be taken and the other will be left" (Lk 17:34–35). Again, the invitation is to consider that any moment could be our last. Thus, meditation on death serves a value for Christians similar to that it serves for Buddhists.

I've made only a few adaptations to this meditation from the way I learned it as a Tibetan Buddhist. The two fundamental points for contemplation are the certainty of death and the uncertainty of when death will come, truths as valid for Christians as for Buddhists. My changes include adding a point at the beginning about putting ourselves in the presence of God, reminding ourselves that we are engaged in a dialogic process with God, not a solitary activity, and shifting the focus from a motivation to attain Enlightenment to a motivation to work for God's kingdom.

The instruction near the end of the Buddhist meditation is framed almost solely in terms of devoting more time to meditation. For Christians, time with God in individual prayer and reflection is crucial, a necessary part of our spiritual growth. But we are also meant to be Christ in the world, and how we behave toward others is an important part of being adequately prepared for death. My instructions in that last part of the meditation reflect that fact.

It is easy to appreciate how a deeper awareness that death can occur at any time can have a positive impact not only on our motivation for prayer, but other aspects of our lives as well. If we're on bad terms with someone, it is so easy to think there will always be time to make amends. It is so easy for us to put off a visit to a parent or a sick friend thinking there will always be future opportunities to see them. So easy for us to procrastinate on important projects, convincing ourselves there is no need to do today what we can put off until tomorrow. If we truly appreciated that there may not be a tomorrow, our behavior would certainly be different.

The most important thing in doing this meditation is to do it with serious concentration. Like many of the meditations I present here the ultimate conclusion is a straightforward one that we have no difficulty comprehending. We all know that we will die someday and as an intellectual matter we all "know" that death can come for us at any moment. The problem is that we don't internalize this realization. We live as though it were not a reality. What we are seeking is to turn the intellectual understanding into a level of realization that permeates our entire being so that we may live more mindfully and purposefully.

I have friends whose son has a very serious peanut and tree nut allergy. The slightest amount of nut product risks an anaphylactic shock that could kill him. In the course of a discussion about what effect it might have on someone to know that he had only a few months to live, the boy calmly said, "I have a peanut allergy. I never know any day if I will be alive tomorrow." That is the kind of strong awareness of the imminence and unpredictability of death I am talking about, and attaining that requires a deliberateness and seriousness of purpose in doing the meditation, not skimming through and thinking, "Oh, I already know that."

Another exercise I learned as a Tibetan Buddhist may sound a bit strange. The idea was to pick a tree on the path some distance away from where you are standing and see that tree as the point of your death. You then walk slowly toward it, with each step recognizing that you are one step closer to death. If you say, "There's death" and walk toward it with no concentration or feeling, that is a waste of time. But if you can really in a concentrated way see the tree as death, it is possible to generate a deep feeling—sometimes of fear, sometimes another emotion—when doing the exercise. Again this is the reason that combining stabilization and analytical meditations is so important.

You might give this exercise a try sometime when you are out walking. The object could be anything—a building some distance away in the direction in which you are walking...the end of a street...some other landmark. Anything will serve as a workable "end point." As with the meditation, the aim is to gain a deeper realization that our death can occur at any moment.

Chapter 15

Overcoming Anger and Developing Patience

It is very easy to see that anger too is a form of suffering. There is nothing comfortable about it. Anger generates a hardness in the heart, general restlessness, and all the associated disadvantages of a cruel mind. Quite obviously it leads to nothing but pain.

Lama Yeshe and Lama Zopa Rinpoche, *Wisdom Energy*

THE MEDITATION

Begin by asking God for the grace to develop the ability to deal with anger without causing harm to others, and to develop greater patience and love so that your heart may become free from anger.

First, develop an awareness of anger arising—of the physical sensations and the thoughts that appear in your mind when you get angry. Call to mind some event in the recent past where someone hurt you or someone else or otherwise did something that caused you to become angry. Put yourself back in the situation and allow the anger to arise. Really let yourself feel it, becoming aware of how it feels in both your body and your mind. Do not judge or evaluate the feeling, simply be aware of it.

Next, spend some time contemplating the fruits of anger. Start by considering your own physical and mental suffering: what happens to you both mentally and physically when anger arises?

Consider also how anger disturbs the peace and happiness of everyone around you. Consider all of the negative things that flow from anger, how it sometimes causes people to become actually sick, how easily it causes us to say or do things we later regret and are ashamed of, how it pushes aside our impulse to love. Call to mind times when your own anger has caused you to say or do things that have hurt another person or where your negative energy seemed to poison the air around you. Or call to mind a situation where someone else's anger has led them to say or do something that hurt another.

As you contemplate those painful fruits of anger, develop in your mind a strong desire to let only love fill your heart, to be able to recognize anger when it arises and find ways to dissipate it that do not bring harm to yourself or to others.

Now go back to the strong feeling of anger that you generated. Again, really allow the feeling of anger to arise so that it suffuses your being. When it does, pray with one or more of the following "antidotes" to anger.

> Note: Pick any combination of the following suggestions and spend time with them. Do not try to do them all in one sitting. If you do more than one in a single sitting, as you end the first, before turning to a second one, again allow the feeling of anger you generated at the outset of the meditation to rise strongly.

Arrow/target. Consider that all effects have a cause. Something caused the other person to act in a hurtful way toward you. Ask yourself:

Did I do something that prompted the act or word that made me angry?

Even if there was no intent on my part to create bad feeling, can I see something, anything, in my behavior—in my words or action—that might have provoked it?

If there was something I did or said, even if it was unintentional, even if it seemed innocent to me, isn't that a reason to refrain from anger at the reaction it provoked?

Stick. When someone hits you with a stick, do you get angry at the stick? Why not? Isn't it because you recognize that the stick is not the true cause of the injury inflicted on you?

Consider who the real villain is, when someone behaves badly toward you. Isn't it the delusion in the other's own mind? Realize that a person who harms you is acting under the control of anger, attachment, or ignorance. If someone is completely overwhelmed by delusion, how can you be angry at him?

It is as though the person were suffering from mental illness. If you were harmed by someone who was mentally ill, would you be angry? Wouldn't you recognize her action for what it was—the product of an illness?

Isn't compassion the only possible response toward such a person? Can you look at the other person's suffering, rather than your own, so as to allow compassion to arise in your heart?

The person who harms you is like a horse being led by another, or a stick wielded by another. As Santideva says

If I become angry with the wielder
Although I am actually harmed by his stick,
Then since he too is secondary, being in turn incited by hatred,
I should really be angry with his hatred.[1]

Standing in the shoes of the other. Get a firm picture in your mind of the person who has made you angry, who hurt you by word or deed.

When you feel the anger, where is the focus of your attention? It is on you, isn't it?

Put your focus on the one whose action or words created the situation and ask, where did it come from? What is the pain or the fear or the insecurity that caused the person to say or do the thing that you find irritating or offensive?

What would it be like to experience that pain or fear or insecurity? Put yourself in a situation where you experience those feelings. What does it feel like?

Reflect on these words of Atticus Finch in *To Kill a Mockingbird*:

> If you can learn a simple trick, you'll get along a lot better with all kinds of folks. You never understand a person until you consider things from his point of view...until you climb into his skin and walk around in it.... You never really know a man until you stand in his shoes and walk around in them.[2]

Can you take that advice?

What happens when you look at things from inside the skin or shoes of the other? Can you understand more about the person's behavior if you take the focus off yourself and your pain and put it on the other?

The precious teacher. Ask yourself: if everyone were always good and kind to you, when would you get to test your patience? How would you develop patience and gain control over the delusions that arise in your mind?

Isn't it true that the difficult situations we face are the ones that do the most for our spiritual growth? Doesn't that make the person who harms you effectively your teacher? Someone who gives you a chance to learn and grow?

Santideva says that "because I am able to practice patience with him, [the person who makes me angry] is worthy of being given the very first fruits of my patience, for in this way he is the cause of it."[3]

Sit with Santideva's words until you can feel at least some feeling of gratitude toward the person who caused your anger.

The effect of death. The focus here is simple: Consider that you or the person you are angry with could die now.

How will you feel if the person dies while you are in the grip of angry feelings toward them? With no ability to rectify things? No chance to develop a more positive feeling toward him?

If you were to die, would you want to die with anger in your heart?

Impermanence. Recall the meditation on impermanence. Everything changes, moment by moment.

The anger or delusion that caused the other to behave badly toward you is impermanent.

Your own feeling of anger is impermanent.

Whatever harm the person caused to you is impermanent.

The situation will change—everything about the current situation will change—so why get upset over it? Why allow your mind to be disturbed over it? Why allow your peace to be shattered by something that is changeable?

Simple logic. There are only two possibilities. Either you have some ability to affect the situation or person who has caused you anger or you do not. So the question to reflect on is a simple one:

If you can change the situation, why get angry, why not make the change?

If you cannot change the situation, why get angry? What good will the anger do? What can it possibly accomplish?

As you reflect, recall the words of the Serenity Prayer:

> God grant me the serenity to accept the things I cannot change;
> Courage to change the things I can;
> And wisdom to know the difference.[4]

*   *   *

After you have spent some time on one or more of these "antidotes," look again at the person who is the object of your anger. Can you look upon him or her any more softly than you did at the outset?

Reflect on these words spoken by the Dalai Lama to a Christian audience:

> God created you as an individual and gave you the freedom to act in a way that is compatible and in accordance with the Creator's wishes—to act in an ethical way, in a moral way, and to live a life of an ethically disciplined, responsible individual. By feeling and practicing tolerance and patience toward fellow creatures, you are fulfilling that wish: you are pleasing your Creator. That is, in a way, the best gift, the best offering you can make to the divine Creator.[5]

Now spend some time trying to generate a feeling of love toward the person with whom you were angry. You may consider doing some tong-len (chapter 6) with that person as your focus, or using the person as an object in the meditation on inexhaustible love (chapter 10). Try affirmatively to replace your feelings of anger toward him or her with feelings of compassion.

Once you can feel compassion toward the person, can you also bring yourself to forgive? See what happens when you mentally express words of repentance toward the person.

As you near the end of your prayer period, look back and see where you were able to loosen some of your feelings of anger and what hindrances arose. Talk to God about both of them.

COMMENTARY

One of the most difficult challenges for a Christian is Christ's command that we love our enemies, not only those who are good and kind to us. It is natural for anger, rather than love, to arise in our hearts when someone hurts us or someone we love by word or deed.

In Buddhism, anger is one of the root delusions from which all other delusions flow. Overcoming anger is thus very important in the Tibetan tradition. Lama Thubten Zopa Rinpoche spoke of this in terms that are useful for a Christian to reflect on:

> As long as there is anger in the mind, it is possible to have an enemy. If there is no possibility for anger in the mind, if anger does not arise, no enemy is possible. Whether you have an enemy or not depends on whether you have anger or not. Even if everyone is bad to you, everyone is angry at you, if you have no anger in your mind, you cannot find even one enemy among these people. If one's mind is full of compassion and loving kindness toward all beings, even if everyone harms you, from your side you see everyone as a friend.[6]

Thus, we must strive to overcome anger and develop patience, which here means the patience of being indifferent to harms (real or perceived) inflicted by others and of voluntarily accepting hardships. Tibetan teaching is that unless we develop patience in bearing hardships, we cannot be successful in spiritual practice.

Rooted in compassion, the teaching is that one should be particularly patient of harm inflicted by others.

In the Tibetan tradition, a number of "antidotes" are used to help overcome anger and develop patience. I offer several of them in this meditation. You might find one or more that resonate strongly with you. When you do, they can become your first line of attack when you feel anger start to arise.

We begin the meditation, as usual, by asking for a grace. I then suggest that you allow a feeling of anger to arise in you—to see it for what it is and label it for what it is. This is a particularly important step for Christians. Buddhists find it easier to accept that feelings rise and vanish and are not "good" or "bad" in themselves. Many Christians have been taught that they should not feel anger, that anger is a sin. Thus there is a tendency to deny it when it occurs. We cannot, however, address something effectively if we don't acknowledge its existence.

There is also value in spending some time really seeing and experiencing the effects of anger when it arises. It is especially important to understand how anger can so cloud your mind that you completely lose any sense of God's love and presence in such moments. The mind can become so filled with anger that there is no space for anything else.

While the antidotes I present are fairly self-explanatory, let me say a few words about some of them.

The *arrow/target* reflection is rooted in the Buddhist concept of karma, a Sanskrit word that means mental activity. The term is used most commonly to refer to the law of cause and effect. Karma is one way of understanding the fundamental Buddhist teaching that all things exist as "dependent arisings," that is, that all things arise in dependence on causes and conditions. The major point to understand is that negative actions generate negative results and positive actions generate positive results. Our tendency when someone behaves badly toward us is to think the problem comes from him entirely. We put the blame on the other, thinking he is the problem. When that happens, we label the other enemy and that is how our mind sees him. The invitation here is simply to consider the reality that I may have done something that provoked the angry reaction in another that led to him harming me. That if I had not done something to create the cause, the other person would not be acting in this way.

This is not a way of thinking unique to Tibetan Buddhism. Part of the fourth step of the Twelve Step program involves looking at your own part in the wrongs committed against you by others. The *Big Book* of Alcoholics Anonymous speaks of "resolutely look[ing] for our own mistakes." It encourages us to look to ask, "where had we been selfish, dishonest, self-seeking and frightened? Though a situation had not been entirely our fault, we tried to disregard the other person involved entirely. Where were we to blame?"[7]

My high school debate coach had a rule that we were not allowed to blame the judge when we lost a round. We were never permitted to say the judge was biased or made a mistake or any other variation on those themes that might excuse our losing a ballot. The reality was that there were some really bad judges and they sometimes made bad decisions. There were also some judges who were nowhere near objective. Nonetheless, my coach was wise to recognize that once we started blaming judges for our losses, it would be easy to get into the habit of making excuses. And that habit and those excuses would prevent us from examining seriously what we could have done better.

There are doubtless many times when we have done nothing to provoke some word or action by another person that hurts us. But our first response can't be to find someone else to blame. It has to be to look inward, not to blame or beat up on ourselves, but simply to examine what we might have done differently.

What I term the *stick* reflection combines two Tibetan approaches—one that sees the person with whom you are angry as a stick and the other that sees him as a mental patient. I combine them because both help us understand that the person who hurts us is not acting with a controlled mind. We tend to see the other person and his or her anger or other negative state as one and the same. The goal is to develop an understanding that the two are not one, but rather, that the other person is acting out of his or her own delusion and suffering. If we can see others as completely overwhelmed by their own negative state, it is easier for compassion to arise.

This, too, finds resonance with the Twelve Step approach. The *Big Book* of Alcoholics Anonymous talks about the value of realizing that "the people who wronged us were perhaps spiritually sick. Though we did not like their symptoms and the way these disturbed us, they, like ourselves, were sick too." We are encouraged to pray for the ability to show those who wrong us "the same tolerance, pity, and patience that we would cheerfully grant a sick friend," saying to ourselves, "This is a sick man. How can I be helpful to him?"[8]

One might counter by saying we ought to demand more from others, that treating them the way one might treat a sick person ignores that they may actually behave that way by choice. What comes to mind in response is another saying of Santideva: "Even if it were the nature of the childish to cause harm to other beings, it would still be incorrect to be angry with them. For this would be like begrudging fire for having the nature to burn."[9] Our anger serves no purpose.

Standing in the shoes of the other is also not a distinctively Buddhist idea, as the words of Atticus Finch convey. It does, however, form part of this meditation in its traditional form. It is natural to look at things from our own standpoint, but this often blinds us to the standpoint of others. To the extent that we can train ourselves to stand back and consider where the other person is coming from, so to speak, we can diffuse many difficult situations.

Often our anger stems, not from some intentional harmful act committed by another, but from some misunderstanding or an inadvertent act of another. Looking at the situation from the other person's standpoint may help us to more easily see when this is the case, which itself might help our anger to dissipate.

The *precious teacher* is based on the idea that it is impossible to practice patience with those who are good to us. When I reflect on this, what always comes to mind is Jesus' saying in St. Matthew's Gospel that if we limit our love to only those who love us or greet only our brothers, we are doing nothing exceptional. The real trick is to carry over those attitudes to those who are not good to us. Only if we are exposed to such people can we develop this ability.

The person who gives us harm is also a test of how far we have grown spiritually. We sometimes feel as if we've made a certain amount of progress. If we are never tested, we can easily live in the delusion that we've come further than we have. The person who behaves badly toward us provides a reality check as to where we are.

The *effect of death* reflection is a particularly powerful one for me. I know people who live unhappily with the fact that they never made amends with someone who has since died, with whom they were on bad terms. And I have had family members die who were not on bad terms with me, but whose death left me feeling that I had not said to them things I wish I had said. So when anger arises, it is easy for me quickly to remind myself that I would not want this to be the last emotion I felt toward a person if one or the other of us died.

I made only minor changes to these antidotes from the way I learned them. As originally presented, they are equally useful for

---

Christians and Buddhists. Apart from my combination of two antidotes into the *stick* reflection, my only change was to add some texts for reflection.

I suggest that in a single prayer period you try one or perhaps two of these, after which you might engage in some practice designed to replace the feeling of anger with one of compassion. Over time, you will develop a sense of which ones are helpful to you and call on them when a situation of anger arises.

If you develop a strong affinity for the antidote in a meditative setting, you will find it easy to call to mind "on the spot" when anger arises. In an actual situation in which strong anger arises, the Tibetan instruction is to turn into stone—say and do nothing, to give the mind a chance to calm, the equivalent of counting to ten. Then in a calmer state, apply one of the antidotes.

Whatever antidote or antidotes you use in the meditation, you should end by spending some time trying to look with compassion at the object of your anger. Once you can do that, focus on whether you can bring yourself to forgive the wrong that has been done to you. Forgiveness is a very difficult thing, but it is demanded of us as Christians. "Forgive us our trespasses as we forgive those who trespass against us," as the Lord taught us to pray. The antidotes may help us develop a more forgiving heart.

For all but the most spiritually advanced, these antidotes are not likely to be effective in confronting a grievous offense. The reality, however, is that what trips us up on a daily basis tend to be smaller grievances. Against those, these strategies can be very effective. And the more we train our minds in compassion and forgiveness, the more compassionate and forgiving we will be in the face of more serious offenses.

Chapter 16

Eight Worldly Concerns

If you check your life, you will see from your own experience that happiness and suffering are dependent upon your mind, upon your interpretation. They do not come from outside, from others. All of your happiness and all of your suffering are created by you, by your own mind.

Lama Thubten Zopa Rinpoche,
Transforming Problems into Happiness

THE MEDITATION

Begin by asking for the grace to develop a stance of renunciation, abandoning the temptations of temporal, worldly concerns, so that you may devote yourself without distraction to laboring with Christ for the coming of his Kingdom.

One by one, reflect on each of the Eight Worldly Concerns (presented here in four pairs) and consider how much of your behavior is motivated by attachment toward one or aversion toward the other. Spend time on each, thinking of examples of how they arise in your life as you reflect on the questions that follow.

(1) *Craving for happiness dependent on the sensory pleasures and* (2) *aversion to suffering and problems relating to sensory experiences.*

How do I react when the food served to me is not as tasty as I would like? Or when the temperature outside is too hot or too cold? Or when my body aches? Or when I'm sitting or standing next to someone with an unpleasant body odor?

How does it feel when I experience a craving for a certain food? Or for some new product I desire?

Bring to mind a concrete example of a very pleasant sensory experience, and then a very unpleasant one. What goes on, not just in your body, but also in your mind when you experience a craving for the pleasant experience or an aversion to the unpleasant one? How do such feelings affect you?

(3) *Craving for praise and admiration and* (4) *fear of blame and criticism.*

How do I feel when someone praises or compliments me for something I've done? Or the way I look?

How do I react when I am blamed, especially if I think the blame is undeserved? How do I react to criticism?

Call to mind an instance when you were praised or complimented effusively and then a time when you were blamed unjustly. What do you feel when you picture those occasions? Again, pay attention to what goes on both in your body and your mind.

(5) *Craving to obtain material possessions and* (6) *fear of losing, or not obtaining, material possessions.*

What role do my possessions play in my happiness?

How much time do I spend worrying about whether something will happen to one or another of my possessions?

How do I feel when I can't have something that I want to possess or use?

Call to mind first, a situation where a possession that mattered to you was lost, stolen, or broken, and then a situation where you couldn't have something you really wanted. What do you feel when you call such situations to mind? What does it feel like in your body? In your mind?

(7) *Craving to hear agreeable ideas and to have a good reputation, and* (8) *aversion to hearing contrary ideas and experiencing dishonor.*

How important is it that other people think well of me? Do I worry about my reputation?

How do I react when people disagree with me? When their ideas are a rejection of my own?

What does it feel like?

Now reflect on whether your attachments or aversions to the Eight Worldly Concerns have brought you any lasting happiness. Ask yourself:

For how long am I satisfied when I get exactly what I want to eat or drink? When the temperature is just right?

How much lasting satisfaction do I get from the praise of another? How long is it before I'm hoping to receive more praise?

For how long do any of my possessions make me happy? Are there possessions that were once very important to me but that now sit in the back of a closet somewhere?

Next consider the consequences of our attraction to the Eight Worldly Concerns. How much peace is there in my mind if I'm constantly shifting between happiness at being praised and unhappiness at criticism? Or between happiness when I am given tasty food and unhappiness when the food is not as good? Or between happiness when I receive a new possession and unhappiness when it breaks? Reflect on how attachment to the Eight Worldly Concerns keeps your mind constantly up and down, never at peace.

Think of examples of how attachment to the Eight Worldly Concerns has led you, or tempted you, to commit negative acts of body, speech, and mind. Do you ever feel the need to criticize someone else in order to build yourself up? Are you more likely to praise others or blame them? Does concern for your material possessions make you less giving and more selfish than you could be? Think of other examples.

Consider how attachment to the Eight Worldly Concerns causes mental agitation. Think of how easily you get upset when you cannot get your keys out of your pocket... the Internet goes down... you can't find your cell phone... you can't find a parking space. All of this agitation stems from the Eight Worldly Concerns.

Consider that our attachment to pleasurable things and aversion to unpleasant things prevent us from attaining ultimate happiness and freedom from suffering, by keeping us focused on things that can bring no lasting satisfaction.

Reflect on these words of Santideva:

> Where would I possibly find enough leather
> With which to cover the surface of the earth?
> But (wearing) leather just on the soles of my shoes
> Is equivalent to covering the earth with it.
> Likewise it is not possible for me
> To restrain the external course of things;
> But should I restrain this mind of mine
> What would be the need to restrain all else?[1]

Understand that outward difficulties are endless; the only way to overcome them is to relinquish attachment and aversion to temporal, worldly things.

As you bring your prayer to a close, spend some time talking with Jesus about where you are particularly pulled by worldly concerns. If there is one of the eight concerns that is a particular problem for you, talk about that with Jesus, asking how you may gain the strength to overcome it.

COMMENTARY

We may think we are devoting sufficient attention to spiritual practice, but if our minds are preoccupied with worldly concerns, we will make little spiritual progress. Tibetan lamas often warn their students that it is easy to recite mantras, make offerings, and do many other things that look like serious practice, all the while thinking of the material things of the world.

The Eight Worldly Concerns function as distractions from our spiritual growth and prevent us from having any peace. Lama Thubten Zopa Rinpoche calls them the source of all of our problems in life. When we are under their control, our mental state becomes like a ball on water, constantly bobbing in this direction or that. There is no peace. Everything others do causes our mind to shift in one direction or another. It is necessary to develop a mind of renunciation, freed from attachment to temporal, worldly things.

Buddhists and Christians share the understanding that renunciation does not mean we cannot enjoy the things of the world. The point is not that we should give up our homes and our possessions, but rather that we need to embrace the reality that neither they nor anything else of this world brings lasting satisfaction. The problem is not the objects of our enjoyment or repulsion, but the clinging to them that we experience.

Before we can commit to a path that seeks to overcome the Eight Worldly Concerns, we must really be convinced of their danger. Their pull is incredibly strong, but we are often unaware of them when they arise. Thus, the first step of the meditation is to recognize the extent to which we are subject to these attractions and aversions. Because they tend to operate unconsciously, it is important to spend enough time on this first step, really recognizing how these forces feel when they arise. Calling to mind specific instances will help you to focus on these bodily and mental feelings and make you better able to recognize them when they start to arise.

The second necessary step is to convince yourself at a deep level that the Eight Worldly Concerns do not bring lasting happiness. Lama Yeshe impressed on his students the importance of examining what value they derived from the "material supermarket," suggesting that this is a lifelong task. Hence the instruction to spend time reflecting on the fact that the things to which we are attached bring only temporary satisfaction.

Finally, we need to understand the extent to which our attachment to the Eight Worldly Concerns not only disrupts our peace of mind, but also creates what Buddhists would call negativities and what a Christian would call sin.

From a Buddhist perspective, there will always be a problem as long as we are not aware that the things of this world do not bring lasting happiness. If we remain attached to material possessions, then no matter how much we have, it is not enough. If we retain an aversion to criticism, no matter how many good things people say about us, we will live with fear, resentment, and anticipation of criticism. If we cling to our attachments and aversions, it won't matter how external conditions change. No matter how much we have—friends, possessions, or anything else—there is no satisfaction, no peace. This lesson is no less important for a Christian than for a Buddhist.

From a Christian perspective, the meditation also helps bring forth what St. Ignatius of Loyola termed a state of active indifference—indifference as to whether our experience is what we would conventionally label good or bad, recognizing that we can find God in all things. Ignatius instructs that "we must make ourselves indifferent to all created things, as far as we are allowed free choice and are not under any prohibition. Consequently, as far as we are concerned, we should not prefer health to sickness, riches to poverty, honor to dishonor, a long life to a short one. The same holds for all other things."[2] The idea is that everything has the potential to deepen our life with God.

I never received extensive instruction on how to meditate on the Eight Worldly Concerns. Instead, I received teachings on them at various times, with the message that this was an important subject of meditation and suggestions for points to reflect on. The various points I include in the meditation are drawn from my own reflections on the Eight Worldly Concerns in light of the teaching I received on them. There is very little difference between how a Buddhist would reflect on the points in this meditation and how a Christian would. Apart from beginning by asking for a grace and ending with a colloquy—both of which underscore that as Christians we are engaged in a dialogic process with God—I present the meditation with no changes from how I practiced it as a Buddhist.

Chapter 17

Taking Refuge

When in difficulty, we should turn to the Three Jewels, praying to them with confidence that their power will enable us to solve our problems. If instead we ignore these Objects of Refuge and try to overcome the difficulty by other, worldly means, such as other people or material things, we shall not succeed.

Geshe Rabten, *The Essential Nectar*

THE MEDITATION

Consider the experiences of this life. How you are always experiencing some suffering, some need. Allow to surface the fears, anxieties, and worries you experience almost every day. Realize that even when things are going well, there is something missing; there is a restlessness in you, a lack of satisfaction.

Next, consider all of the methods you use to try to deal with your sufferings—all of the things you turn to when you feel bored, sad, or lacking in self-confidence: your music...movies...books... shopping...food...other pastimes. Do any provide more than temporary distraction? Do any provide a lasting solution, a permanent end to suffering?

Now look at all of the things you do to try to find security and happiness—acquisition of physical possessions...savings in the bank...trips to far-off places. Do any of these bring permanent happiness?

Be aware of how you are constantly moving from one thing to another in an effort to find happiness and to alleviate suffering. Reflect on how they all fall short.

After some time, consider the words of Isaiah: "Why spend your money on what is not bread, your wages on what fails to satisfy?" (Is 55:2). Why, indeed.

Sit with St. Augustine's recognition: "Our hearts are restless, O God, until they rest in you." Feel his words resonate in you as you realize that there is only one place you can go to find complete happiness and satisfaction.

As you hear Augustine's words, visualize God, who breathes us into existence and who continues breathing life into each of us moment by moment until we die. Recognize your absolute dependence on this God who loves you endlessly and unconditionally.

Now visualize in front of you Jesus Christ, seated on a throne, his body resplendent and radiant in his resurrected glory. Standing around him are his mother, Mary, the apostles, and the saints— all of the holy men and women who have gone before us.

Feel the presence of the Holy Spirit, while still keeping in your mind the picture of God and of Jesus surrounded by Mary and the saints.

Visualize all of them looking at you with delight because you are committing yourself to deepen your relationship with God. They all smile at you with encouragement and love.

Now, give voice to your recognition that your ultimate source of refuge is God. Keeping in the background your visualization of Jesus, Mary, and the saints and your sense of the presence of the Holy Spirit, start by visualizing in the front and center of your field of vision God breathing life into you. See yourself held in the loving gaze of God, taking in the breath of God with each inhalation.

As you hold that visualization, pray:

I give my heart, in total trust, to God, the Father Almighty. I take refuge in the almighty love of God. I live in the security that wherever I am, God is there with me.

Next, visualize Christ. Flowing from Christ's heart are rays of brilliant light. The rays from his heart flow through your body, removing all of your negative tendencies of body, speech, and mind, and leaving in their place only Christ's love.

As you hold that visualization, pray:

I give my heart, in total trust, to Jesus Christ. I take refuge in my encounter with God through Christ. I live in the security that I can encounter the divine in human form and that the divine wants to manifest itself in me.

Next, visualize the Holy Spirit in whatever form is most natural for you (a dove, a flame, a wind, an unseen presence). Let yourself feel the Spirit moving through you.

As you hold that feeling, pray:

I give my heart, in total trust, to the Holy Spirit. I take refuge in the reality of the Spirit of God alive in me and in the whole world. I live in the security that the Holy Spirit will stir my heart and lead me to use my life for God's work.

Repeat these prayers as many times as you feel drawn to do so. If you are impelled to speak further words to God, speak them. And then simply sit in the presence of the Trinity, feeling both secure and empowered by that presence.

COMMENTARY

The *Taking Refuge* practice is not technically a Tibetan Buddhist analytical meditation (although it functions very much like one). Rather, refuge is a foundational Buddhist practice, one that lends itself to easy adaptation for Christians.

As described by His Holiness the Dalai Lama, refuge is a state of mind entrusting yourself from the depth of your heart to a superior being. For a Buddhist, the only final refuge is the "Triple Gem," and so Buddhists take refuge in the Buddha, the Dharma, and the Sangha. The source of refuge is the Dharma—the teachings that show the way; the Buddha is the master who shows or teaches the doctrine; the Sangha is the community that provides companionship on the path. One takes refuge in the Buddha as a model to emulate, in the Dharma as the teachings revealed by the enlightened mind, and the Sangha because we need the help and companionship of others along the way.

The basic refuge practice for Tibetan Buddhists begins by developing a conviction that the places we have gone for refuge in the past have never provided more than temporary happiness or relief from suffering. It then moves to a reflection on the qualities of the Buddha, Dharma, and Sangha. It concludes with recitation of a refuge formula, accompanied by a visualization of the "Triple Gem," as a physical expression of what is felt inside, of the unbearableness of the suffering experienced by you and all sentient beings and the desire to end that suffering.

Christians do not speak of "taking refuge" in the same way, but there are many biblical references to God as refuge. And as Christians, we engage in something very similar to what Buddhists do when they take refuge when we express our trust and faith in the Trinity, recognizing that God alone is the source of our strength, peace, and happiness. To be very clear, I am not suggesting a one-to-one correspondence between the threefold embodiment of Buddhahood in the Buddha, Dharma, Sangha, and the Christian Trinitarian understanding of three persons in one God. I have known people to engage in torturous attempts to pair the two in one fashion or another and I find no value in such efforts.

Rather, I am suggesting that our refuge in the Trinity serves a purpose for Christians similar to that of Buddhists taking refuge in the Triple Gem. Rowan Williams analogizes the words at the beginning of the Apostles' Creed to the Buddhist refuge formula: Just as a Buddhist saying, "I take refuge in the Buddha" says, "The Buddha is where I belong," that which "I have confidence in to keep me safe," the Christian expression of belief in God the Father Almighty "is the beginning of a series of statements about where I find anchorage of my life, where I find solid ground, home."

Thus, this seems to me a very useful practice for Christians. I'm not the first to have this thought. As I was finalizing this book, the director of the Lama Yeshe Wisdom Archive sent me a collection of lectures given by Lama Yeshe at Kopan Monastery during the Christmas season in 1975. In one of them, he said that he had at certain times given the refuge ceremony to Christians "in accordance with their own devotional experience,"[1] encouraging them to build their visualization around their devotion to Jesus.

In adapting the refuge practice, I retain the basic structure of the Buddhist meditation.

The first step involves considering all the places we look for refuge. This is not difficult: We have been taking refuge all of our lives. Since birth we have taken refuge in many different things for comfort and protection—our parents, our spouse or significant other, our friends, books, travel, food, prized possessions. It is fine to rely on all of those things for limited purposes, but none can be our ultimate refuge because none brings complete and permanent happiness and freedom from suffering. Recognizing their limitation, we want to sit with a sense of our need for God and the dawning recognition of the fact that only God can bring lasting happiness and peace. One way of accomplishing this first step is to engage in a short version of the *Eight Worldly Concerns* meditation (chapter 16).

This first step is important: we are not taking refuge out of fear or feeling that any port in the storm will do. We take refuge in God because we recognize that God is the source of our strength, peace, and happiness. That only God can give us what we truly need.

This is the essence of poverty of spirit, the first of the Beatitudes (Mt 5:1–12), which recognizes our complete dependence on God. Johannes Baptist Metz calls this first Beatitude "not just another virtue, one among many," but "a necessary ingredient in any authentic Christian attitude toward life. Without it there can be no Christianity and no imitation of Christ."[2] We continually seek to grow in the conviction of our need for, and absolute dependence on, God and our recognition that nothing except God can bring us lasting peace and happiness. St. Augustine's oft-repeated words express it well: "Our hearts are restless until they rest in you."

After this initial step is the actual refuge practice, which involves both visualization and a verbal prayer. The prayer I offer reflects the influence of Brother David Steindl-Rast, especially his book *Deeper Than Words: Living the Apostles' Creed*, an apt title for these purposes in that one can view the three parts of the refuge prayer taken together as simply an alternative way of praying our creed. Brother David emphasizes that the creed is an expression of faith, not intellectual assent. What we profess in the creed is that to which we give our hearts, that which orients our lives, not a checklist of beliefs. The prayer in the meditation also reflects Brother David's way of talking about the Father, the Son, and the Holy Spirit, because his words speak to my heart.

Tibetan Buddhist teachers recommend repeating the refuge prayer many times, each time trying to make the visualization stronger and to deepen the interior thought of refuge. Thus I recommend that you repeat the prayer as many times as you are drawn to do before adding whatever other prayer you wish to make to God.

People sometimes ask Buddhists what is the value of formally taking refuge. A Christian could also ask the same, "I already know I believe, so why engage in this prayer?" Indeed, many Christians recite a creed every week in services of worship. The ritual act, though, has meaning. It is a reminder both of the ultimate unsatisfactoriness of the things in which we usually take refuge and what it means as a Christian to commit oneself to God.

Taking refuge is not just about reciting words. We don't take refuge and then sit back and wait for God to take care of everything for us. The words and the meditation are meant to signify a responsibility and a commitment to live our lives in a certain way. A Buddhist taking refuge is committing to live by certain precepts and follow the path to liberation. The same is true for Christians. If I am declaring my refuge in the Trinity, that must translate into a commitment to live my life in a particular way. The behavior won't be perfect. But it is not enough to mouth words that don't impact how we live our lives.

Tibetan lamas teach that how much one gets out of the refuge process depends on one's faith in the objects of refuge. Thus, the Buddhist instruction suggests that one take time to reflect on the characteristics of the Buddha, Dharma, and Sangha before engaging in the recitation of the refuge prayer. You may wish to do the same, spending some time reflecting on your faith in Father, Son, and Holy Spirit, particularly focusing on the qualities you associate with each person of the Trinity.

The recitation of the refuge prayer is both a reflection of our faith and way of deepening it. The same is true of the Apostles' or Nicene Creed—they are expressions of the faith we already have and at the same time our mindful recitation of the creeds helps grow our faith. Done mindfully, this refuge practice can be a very powerful one.

As a final note, like Christians, Buddhists emphasize an ongoing practice of respect toward the objects of refuge. Thus, for example, Buddhist teaching is that images of the Buddha should not be tossed on the floor or otherwise be treated with disrespect. The same is true for Buddhist texts, which should not be used, for example, to sit on or prop up one's computer monitor. This was greatly emphasized in the Tibetan Buddhist communities in which I lived in Nepal and India. At a retreat center in India at which I spent much time, outside of the outhouse there was a hook on which one would hang one's prayer beads (which are typically blessed by a lama) before going to use the toilet. We carried our books from place to place wrapped in cloth coverings and never placed them directly on the floor. What underlies such teachings and practices is respect for our ultimate Refuge. The regular practice of *Taking Refuge* helps keep one mindful about ways we do or do not manifest that respect.

Chapter 18

Seeing Ourselves as Christ

Now with God's help, I shall become myself.

Søren Kierkegaard, *Papers and Journals*

THE MEDITATION

Begin by recognizing that you are in the presence of God, and asking God for the grace to become more fully yourself—to become as God created you to be, and for the grace to be Christ to others in the world.

Visualize Jesus standing in front of you. His face shines "like the sun" and his body is radiant and brilliant, "white as the light," as it appeared to the disciples when Jesus was transfigured before them (Mt 17:2–3).

In the center of the brilliant whiteness of Jesus' chest, his heart is visible. One hand gestures toward his heart, while the other is held out in welcoming embrace.

One of Jesus' feet is in front of the other, ready to move in whatever direction is necessary to bring his love and healing touch to those in need. His eyes are focused intently on you, even as he also takes in all of the other people in all directions, conscious of all of their needs.

Spend time concentrating on the visualization, getting a clear picture of Jesus in your mind.

Now, contemplate the qualities of Jesus you wish to bring forth in yourself:

His nondiscriminating love, poured out for all beings, regardless of their merit or desert.

His generous forgiveness of all those who wronged him, even those who put him to death.

His expansive generosity, feeding thousands, healing person after suffering person.

His inclusive friendship and sense of community that welcomed tax collectors and prostitutes to his table.

His openness to the will of his Father, even when carrying out that will was very difficult.

Spend time on these qualities, allowing examples of Jesus' behavior to surface in your mind. Watch his dealings with other people. If there are other qualities of Jesus you admire and wish particularly to bring forth in yourself, spend time reflecting on those as well.

Now generate a strong desire to be Christ to others in the world, to be the hands and feet of Christ to others, the love and compassion of Christ to all of those in need. Develop the wish that others might look at you and see the face of Christ.

Gazing at Jesus standing before you, as you have visualized him, make a prayer to Jesus from your heart, asking him to rise in you, to fill you with his presence.

See Jesus respond by sending streams of light into you. First, he sends streams of white light from his forehead to yours, eliminating all obstacles and hindrances to your becoming like him. Allow the white light to enter your forehead and flow throughout your entire body, washing away all negativities of body, speech, and mind.

Now from his heart, Jesus' love and compassion come to you in the form of rays of brilliant red light that flow directly into your heart. Feel your heart expand with Jesus' love.

Next, rays of piercing blue light flow from Jesus' eyes to your eyes. As the light flows in, feel your eyes become like Jesus' eyes, able to take in people in all directions no matter how far away, and discern what their needs are.

From Jesus' hands and feet, yellow light flows and is absorbed into your hands and feet as you take in his willingness to provide for the needs of others, even when it is difficult to do.

As the lights continue to flow, feel your desire for Jesus to come closer and closer to you, as you realize you want nothing to separate you from him.

Now see Jesus coming closer and closer to you until there is no separation between him and you. Feel his presence throughout your entire being. Really feel yourself taking on the qualities of Jesus that you emulate. Stay in that space as long as you can.

When the power of the visualization fades, end by praying to Jesus that you may be his presence in the world. To be his body in the world...his eyes...his hands and feet. Pray that when others see you, it is the face of Jesus that they see...that when they feel your touch, it is the touch of Jesus that they feel...that when they feel your love, it is Jesus' love that they feel.

As you bring the meditation to a close, feel Jesus' joy that this is your desire.

COMMENTARY

All of the Buddha's teachings fall into two categories: sutra and tantra. Both have the same aim, but the tantrayana (the path of tantra) is seen by some as a quicker path than the sutrayana, which seeks a more gradual process of thought transformation. All of the meditations I have presented up to now are derived from the sutrayana.

This meditation is adapted from the tantrayana, a subject about which there is much misunderstanding among those without a deep familiarity with Buddhism (or Hinduism, which also has a tantric tradition).

To explain tantric practice in simplest terms (and you can find books and books on tantra, including the wonderful *Introduction to Tantra: A Vision of Totality*, by Lama Yeshe), the idea is to learn to think and act as if we were already fully enlightened—to bring into the present moment those qualities we seek to develop in ourselves. In tantra the practitioner trains herself to view herself and others as divine beings—as transcendentally beautiful and possessing the qualities of enlightenment. The aim is to dissolve the ordinary perception of the self and others, replacing it with the body and soul of the deity. It is thought that the more we learn to see ourselves as a deity, the less bound we will be to the ordinary delusions under which we typically operate.

The various deities involved in tantric practice embody different aspects of Buddha nature and have different roles in guiding the practitioner to enlightenment; each represents different essential qualities of an enlightened being. Lama Yeshe explains

To use the language of psychology, such a deity is an archetype of our own deepest nature, our most profound level of consciousness. In tantra we focus our attention upon such an archetypal image and identify with it in order to arouse the deepest, most profound aspects of our being and bring them into our present reality. It is a simple truth that if we identify ourselves as being fundamentally pure, strong, and capable we will actually develop these qualities, but if we continue to think of ourselves as dull and foolish, *that* is what we will become.[1]

In the early stages, the process of seeing oneself as a deity seems to be (and is) somewhat artificial. But it is believed that over time practitioners will come to perceive the qualities of the deity with greater clarity and move more quickly toward attaining those qualities.

In addition to visualizing oneself as the deity, the tantra practice involves recitation of prayers and the development of the desire to send the blessings of the deity to all sentient beings. Thus, for example, in the practice to Tara (the female aspect of Buddha), Lama Thubten Zopa Rinpoche recommends praying, "Without delay of even a second, may I become Tara and, in each second, free uncountable numbers of sentient beings from all their suffering, and lead them to enlightenment." Then as we visualize Tara being absorbed to our heart, we pray, "My body, speech, and mind have been blessed in Tara's vajra holy body, holy speech, and holy mind."[2]

Tantra was the aspect of Tibetan Buddhist practice for which I had the least affinity. However, as I began looking back over my journals, my notes from various tantric teachings, and books on tantra, I became aware of a striking parallel between Tibetan deity practice and a Christian desire to see oneself as Christ. The Letter to the Philippians instructs, "Have among yourselves the same attitude that is also yours in Christ Jesus" (Phil 2:5), translated by some as "Let this mind be in you that was also in Christ Jesus."

Many years ago, Pope Benedict XVI (while he was still Joseph Ratzinger) wrote that the fact that Jesus became human "shows that he does not regard his divine sonship as something reserved only for himself: the meaning of the incarnation is rather to make what is his available to all."[3] Thus, he says, we "can be 'in Christ,' enter into him and become one with him" and thus share his sonship. We are "planted in the innate Son of the Father (Jn 1:18), with whom we are one single body, one single "seed of Abraham." Ratzinger goes on to say that "to become one with Christ means to lose one's 'oneself,' to cease to regard one's own ego as an absolute," in Buddhist terms, to be less bound to the ordinary delusions that plague us.

On several occasions I have attended a Mass at which, just before the distribution of the Eucharist, the priest held up the bread and wine and said, "Behold what you are. Become what you receive." What is our receipt of the Eucharist, after all, but an element or manifestation of becoming transformed into the body of Christ? We are meant literally to be Christ in the world. The transformation of bread and wine into the body and blood of Christ is the promise—and beginning of the fulfillment—of our own transformation.

Behold what you are. Just as Tibetan Buddhists engage in tantric practice to recognize and bring forth the qualities of the Buddha, which are already there at our core, so too we seek to bring forth our true selves—the qualities of Christ that are already within. And just as Tibetan Buddhists call on the aid of a deity for assistance in revealing their true nature, so too we call on Christ to reveal himself in us.

I have presented the meditation with Christ as the central object, having in mind the imagery often attributed to St. Teresa (but which evidently appear nowhere in her writings):

Christ has no body now but yours,
No hands, no feet on earth but yours
Yours are the eyes through which he looks compassion on
this world
Christ has no body now on earth but yours.

It is possible to further adapt the meditation by changing the central object. Tibetan Buddhists pray with different deities that manifest different qualities of the Buddha. Thus, for example, Manjusri Buddha is associated with wisdom, Chenrezig is the Buddha of loving kindness and compassion, and Tara manifests in twenty-one different aspects (distinguished by color, posture, and adornments) to subdue different obstacles. Christians, particularly Catholic Christians, might engage in the practice using a saint that embodies particular qualities of Christ that they seek to develop.

Many of us feel a special affinity toward particular saints, who are a source of strength for us. In my own case, I think of St. Vincent de Paul, St. Ignatius of Loyola, and St. Joseph. I could easily adapt the practice to use one of those saints as the object of my meditation.

For example, the core Vincentian virtues are zeal, simplicity, gentleness, humility, and self-denial. An adapted meditation using Vincent could include reflection on one or more of those virtues and a visualization in which Vincent sends forth light that fills us with the virtues. You can be as elaborate or as simple as you like. I have at times done a very short form of meditation using Vincent in which I reflect on a particular virtue and then visualize Vincent sending me his energy for that virtue.

Whatever the main object of the meditation, the most important thing, in the words of Lama Yeshe, is "to get a taste, an actual experience, of something that has meaning for you. It doesn't matter how small the piece of chocolate you get is; you taste it."[4] So when you get any actual taste, any strong sensation of the qualities of Christ or the saint you are experiencing, sit with that taste. Allow yourself to really experience it, mining it for all it has to offer you.

Two final comments. First, this practice has significance not only for how we see ourselves, but how we see others. Both

Buddhism and Christianity operate under the (sometimes expressed, sometimes implied) premise that it is hard for us to see in others what we cannot recognize in ourselves. The more we can see Christ's qualities in ourselves, the more easily we will see them in others.

Second, although what I present here is a Christian adaptation, I have read an essay that recounts a discussion between a rabbi and the Dalai Lama that suggests a consonance between tantric practice and the Jewish Shabbat (Sabbath). The rabbi told the Dalai Lama that Shabbat "harkens back to the creation of the world at the same time that it envisions the future messianic redemption." He explained that the Sabbath practices of dressing in fine clothes, setting a beautiful table, and eating fine food anticipate redemption. The Dalai Lama suggested that Shabbat is the Jewish people's visualization exercise. The author of the essay realized that "that is exactly what we do, although we would never see it that way. On Shabbat, we live as though the world were already redeemed, and by so doing, we hasten the cosmic redemption itself."[5] Saying something very similar in nontheological terms, Viktor Frankl spoke of the need to be idealistic in our view of humans, observing that if we take people as they are, we end up making them worse, but that if we overestimate them—if we view them as greater than they may actually now be, we help promote them to what they really can be.

Chapter 19

Meditating on the "I"

Our whole problem is not being aware of the reality of things.
Just like hallucinogenic drugs or mushrooms, wrong conceptions
make our minds hallucinate. We are unable to practice awareness
of reality . . . that what appears to us does not exist in the way that
it appears to exist.

Lama Thubten Zopa Rinpoche, *The Door to Satisfaction*

THE MEDITATION

Begin by recalling that you are in the presence of God on whom your very existence depends. Spend a few minutes focusing on your breath, aware that God is breathing life into you moment by moment.

Generate a strong appearance in your mind of the "I," what appears to you as the self. Call to mind a time when you experienced strong feelings of anger or pride. Steep yourself in the feeling. This should help the "I" to appear strongly.

Now analyze how the "I" appears to you. It seems, doesn't it, that the "I" is independent, not dependent on anything? What you experience is a sense of an autonomous ego. Something concrete, existing in and of itself, separate from your mind and body.

Take the time to see clearly the way the "I" appears to you before moving on. If you lose the sense, go back and generate again a strong feeling of pride or anger and allow the "I" to appear.

Holding onto this strong apprehension of the "I," now ask yourself where it exists. Start to search for it:

Recognize that there are only two possibilities: either the "I" that I have a strong sense of is one with the body and/or mind or it is something completely different from and outside the body or mind. Doesn't that have to be true?

If the "I" exists as one with the body and/or mind, there are three possibilities: the "I" is just the body, the "I" is just the mind, or the "I" is both mind and body.

Spend some time examining how it appears to you. If someone tells you that you're looking good, isn't there an instinctive sense that the "I" is the body?

If you are commended for having had some good idea, isn't there an instinctive sense that "I" am my mind?

Now engage in an analysis to ascertain whether the "I" that appears to me is in fact the body. First, I speak of "my body." When I do, I have a sense of the existence of an "I" to whom the body belongs. Doesn't that imply a distinction between the possessor and that which is possessed? If I possess the body, how can the "I" be the body?

Second, if the "I" is the body, is it the entire body or only part of the body? How does it seem to you? If the "I" is the whole body, how does that relate to the fact that the body is made up of discrete parts? Does the "I" still exist if you lose an arm or a leg? Are all of the parts necessary for the "I" to exist?

If instead the "I" is only part of the body, which part is it? Carefully consider the many parts of the body—arms, legs, flesh, bones, fat, and so on to see whether any one of them is the "I." Continue the analysis until you can see that there is no part of the body that, on examination, is the "I." No part presents itself strongly as a self-existent "I."

Now turn to the mind. Is the "I" the mind? First, I speak of "my mind." If I possess the mind, how can I be the mind?

Second, doesn't the "I" appear to be unitary and permanent? How then could the "I" be the mind, which has many components and changes moment by moment?

Carefully examine the various components of the mind—the sense consciousness, feelings, thoughts, daydreams, desires. Are any of these the "I" that appears to you? If the "I" is one of these parts, which part? Feelings? Desires? Perceptions? Is the "I" your daydreams?

If the "I" is not the body or the mind, perhaps it is both mind and body together. But body and mind are two different things. Doesn't the "I" that appears so strongly to you when you feel anger or pride seem to be of one nature? Doesn't it appear to you as a unitary entity? You don't have the feeling that the "I" you grasp at is made of different natures, do you?

Continue in this vein until you come to a firm conclusion that the "I" that appears to you is not the same as the body and the mind.

The only other possibility is that the "I" exists separately and outside of the mind and body. Can the "I" exist separately from the body and mind? Consider:

I only say "I am sitting," because the body is sitting. When "I am in the room" no part of the "I" is elsewhere. The body and consciousness are in the room. If the "I" were separate from the body and mind, mightn't I be able to say I am in the room even if my body and mind are somewhere else? Is that possible?

Continue until you realize that the "I" cannot exist separately from the body; the "I" must be related to, dependent on the body. Similarly the "I" is related to and dependent on the mind. I say, "I want" something because my mind registers a feeling of desire for it.

There is only one conclusion we can draw from the fact that the "I" is neither the body nor the mind nor separate from them: the "I" does not exist in the way in which it appears to us.

Now allow the false appearance of "I" to disappear. Allow the attachment to that self—the "I" that experiences pride and anger—to disappear. When the false appearance disappears, what remains in the mind is a space like emptiness. Allow yourself to experience the absence of the strong sense of "I."

That space does not mean you are not there. But the "you" that is there is not the sense of "I" that you usually experience. What remains is simply the you God created in God's image and likeness, the you that exists in and for Christ, the you that is Christ in the world.

Now, in that space created by the disappearance of the false sense of the "I," allow Jesus to be present. Ask him to fill the emptiness within you, and feel yourself being suffused with his presence. Realize, in St. Paul's words, that "it is no longer I who live, but Christ lives in me."

Sit for a while with a strong sense of Christ in you.

COMMENTARY

Emptiness is one of the most difficult Buddhist concepts. Yet it cannot be ignored, as it is no exaggeration to say that all Buddhist teaching aims at helping to generate a deep realization of emptiness.

Emptiness, as I discussed in chapter 2, is not annihilation. It is not nonexistence, but rather the nonexistence of things in the way they usually appear to us. Emptiness is a middle ground between the poles of nihilism and of the concrete, permanent existence of persons and things. From a Buddhist perspective all things are empty. The focus in this meditation is on the emptiness of the "I," the fact that the "I" does not exist the way it appears to us.

The Buddhist concept of emptiness is not the same as what Christians mean when we speak of dying to self and rising in Christ, although it has something of that flavor. Despite the fact that the goal for a Christian is different, I see value in this meditation for several interrelated reasons.

First, and most important, it helps soften our attachment to our ego to see that the "I" we have such a strong sense of, and feel such a strong need to protect, is an illusion. Consider the strong sense of ego that arises when someone insults you or is angry at you. The ego feels threatened and we often respond to that threat in some less-than-positive way. Similarly, when we are praised, a strong sense of ego arises, a positive sense that we want to preserve, which again results in behavior that is less than admirable.

For Buddhists, the sense of ego—the feeling of "I" that arises when we are attacked or praised and which causes such suffering—is a manifestation of an innate self-grasping. When we cling to that sense of ego, we experience fear that something will happen to it. The meditation aims to help us soften that strong sense of the "I," and therefore the impulse to act in undesirable ways to protect it. Seeing that the "I" that appears to us does not exist in the way it appears to us to exist helps us loosen our attachment to the "false self."

Second, the meditation offers a way of appreciating our dependence on God. Although the "I" seems like a self-existent, independent entity, we do not, in fact, exist as independent, autonomous beings. Buddhists say the "I" exists in dependence on causes and conditions. We as Christians understand we exist in dependence on God. The meditation helps loosen the sense of an autonomous ego.

Third, the empty space that remains after we dissolve the "I" the false way that it appears leaves room for the rising of Christ. The Christian analogue of emptiness is the space in ourselves that makes room, so to speak, for Jesus to rise in us. To draw attention to that difference, I end the meditation with Paul's assertion that "it is no longer I who live, but Christ lives in me" (Gal 2:20). Whereas the emptiness of Buddhism is absence of personal identity, our Christian identity is defined by communion with Christ (and with each other).

I have made very little adaptation to the way I did this meditation as a Buddhist, except at the beginning and the end. The meditation begins by having us ask for a grace. At the end, I adapted the meditation to allude to our existence in and through Christ and to include the invitation to Jesus to fill the space created by the disappearance of the false self. These changes set the context of our lives as lived in communion with God through Christ.

The emptiness meditation is highly analytical, almost scientific in its approach. In order to benefit from it, however, we can't approach it as merely an intellectual exercise. It is very important to do the analysis with the strong appearance of the "I" the way it appears to our mind. Merely agreeing that the "I" is empty is not enough. We have to understand what it is empty of. The stage of identifying the false view of the "I" that we carry with us is essential.

Essential, but not easy. From birth we have developed the sense of me and not me, of self and of others separate from the self. The "not me" is directly perceptible and strong. The "I," however, does not appear to our mind very strongly, despite our strong belief in its existence. The fact that the "I" does not appear strongly, according to Buddhist teaching, causes fear and anxiety;

not realizing it is an illusion, we grasp at this sense of the "I" in an effort to create a feeling of security.

Because the sense of the "I" is subtle, it takes some prompting for it to arise strongly in the meditation. This is the reason to allow a feeling of anger or pride to rise, because strong emotions like these usually give a good appearance of an independent "I" unrelated to the body and mind. This is especially the case if someone is unjustifiably angry with you—a strong "I" appears then. Similarly, when someone insults you, it provokes a very strong sense that "I" am being attacked. Fear is another emotion that does the same. Any of these strong emotions generates a vividly appearing independent "I."

You may need to do this first stage over and over to generate a clear awareness of this strong sense of an independent "I." Some Tibetan teachers advise their students to do nothing but watch the "I" for weeks or months before proceeding with the rest of the meditation.

Once you get the strong image, allow a part of your mind to hold onto that image and part to investigate it, going through the stages of the analysis. Some Buddhist teachers say you should look at the "I" like a spy because if you look at it too closely, it disappears. Any time during the meditation that you lose a strong sense of the "I," go back again to evoke a strong emotion and allow it to arise again.

PART IV

OTHER MEDITATIONS
AND PRACTICES

Chapter 20

Meditations to Develop Concentration and Mindfulness

My primary focus in this book has been on ways Christians might make use of Tibetan Buddhist analytical meditations. Here I offer a brief look at some other Tibetan (and one non-Tibetan) Buddhist practices.

God seeks to communicate with us always. When we sit down to pray, we don't need to do anything to get God's attention—God is already there waiting for us. The issue is our attentiveness to God's continuous effort to reach us.

Our minds are like undisciplined children, constantly flying off in many directions. You sit down with a book and within a page your mind is thinking about a doctor's appointment you have to make. You are in a meeting listening to someone speak and your mind retreats to a conversation you had that morning, the memory of which reminds you of a movie, which then leads you down a train of thought about a charity supported by the lead actor in that film, and so on.

That lack of discipline carries over into our prayer. We sit in church and, instead of focusing on the reading or sermon we are hearing, our minds go to what we are planning for dinner that evening and what we might need to pick up from the grocery store. We sit for our morning prayer and, while our lips recite one thing, our mind is someplace else.

St. Augustine warned of the need to gain some control over the mind:

> The third commandment [to remember the Sabbath and keep it holy] enjoins quietness of heart, tranquility of mind. This is holiness. Because here is the Spirit of God. This is what a true holiday means, quietness and rest. Unquiet people recoil from the Holy Spirit. They love quarrelling. They love argument. In their restlessness they do not allow the silence of the Lord's Sabbath to enter their lives. Against such restlessness we are offered a kind of Sabbath in the heart. As if God were saying, "Stop being so restless, quiet the uproar in your minds. Let go of all the idle fantasies that fly around in your head." God is saying, "Be still and see that I am God" (Ps. 46). But you refuse to be still. You are like the Egyptians tormented by gnats. The tiniest of flies, always restless, flying about aimlessly, swarm at your eyes, giving no rest. They are back as soon as you drive them off. Just like the futile fantasies that swarm our minds.[1]

Being still is easier said than done. When we begin a prayer practice we quickly realize that we cannot simply will or force ourselves to be attentive and keep our minds from wandering. It takes sustained effort and practice.

When I was a Buddhist, I spent significant periods of time engaged in two forms of Buddhist meditation designed to develop concentration and mindfulness: shamatha and vipassana. Shamatha is frequently practiced by Tibetan Buddhists as a means of stabilizing the mind, and vipassana is a practice of the Theravadan Buddhist tradition. Either can be used at the beginning of any prayer period to develop a state of greater concentration and mindfulness; taking the time to do this will make your subsequent meditation more effective. I talked earlier about the combined use of stabilization and analytical meditation techniques; that same kind of combined use is appropriate with other types of prayer as well, such as traditional *Lectio Divina*, a practice of prayerful reflection on the Bible. At times you might devote an entire prayer period to shamatha or vipassana, helping you develop a silence that leaves you completely open to whatever God wishes to communicate to you.

Both shamatha and vipassana use the breath as a focus of concentration. The breath is a wonderful object of meditation for two reasons. First, you always carry your object of meditation with you. Second, focusing on the rhythm of our breathing naturally centers us. We breathe in, bringing our consciousness to a single spot, and breathe out, letting go of that which troubles and distracts us.

Breathing meditations are well known in the Christian tradition, although they are more common in the Orthodox than the Roman Catholic tradition. I've read instructions by Orthodox contemplatives that strikingly resemble instruction I received in vipassana meditation. Many Christians are familiar with the "Jesus prayer," which is recited in unison with the breath: "Lord Jesus [while inhaling], have mercy on me [while exhaling]." Cardinal Ratzinger likened the use of the breath or the heartbeat in Eastern meditation precisely to this Jesus prayer, which also uses the natural rhythm of the breath, and he acknowledged that this prayer can be of benefit to many people.

Breath is an important image in Christian tradition, and it makes sense that Christians would make use of the breath in their prayer. B. Alan Wallace quotes John of the Cross, who wrote, "The soul that is united and transformed in God breathes God in God with the same divine breathing with which God, while in her, breathes her in himself." These words, Wallace writes, "express the intimate presence of God within each human being by way of the breath, a theme that appears in very early Christian theology. The deepest purpose of the Christian practice of mindfulness of breathing, then, is to make us aware of the dynamic presence of God within our own being."[2]

What follows are some basic instructions in shamatha and vipassana meditation along with some suggestions for how a Christian might make use of them in her prayer.

SHAMATHA

Basic Instruction

The primary focus of concentration in shamatha meditation is the breath. In one common method, the focus is on the sensation of the breath entering and leaving the body through the nostrils.

Sit in a comfortable position that you can hold without frequent adjustments. In this, as in all meditation designed to develop concentration and mindfulness, it is best to keep physical movements to a minimum, which means sitting in a comfortable position that you will be able to maintain for an extended period without moving. In Buddhist communities in Asia, I often saw Westerners try to contort themselves into a full- or half-lotus position, thinking this was the "authentic" way to engage in Buddhist meditation. There is no value in forcing your body into an unnatural and uncomfortable position that you will have to adjust frequently to make yourself more comfortable. By all means sit cross-legged if that is comfortable for you. However, if it is more comfortable to sit upright in a chair with your feet on the ground, that is fine too. The most important thing is to sit upright with a straight back in a way that the flow of your breathing is not impeded. Keep your eyes open, gazing downward at a point about six to eight inches in front of you.

Once you are comfortably seated, focus on the sensation of the breath as it enters and leaves your body through your nose. Don't do anything to try to change your breathing. Breathe normally and simply be attentive to the sensation of the breath coming in and going out.

Inevitably your mind will wander. When it does simply label whatever it was that pulled your mind away from your breath and then return the focus to your breath. By label I mean:

...If you were distracted by a sound, make a mental note, "hearing."

...If you were distracted by a thought, make a mental note, "thinking."

...If you were distracted by a sensation of pain, make a mental note, "pain."

It is sometimes recommended to repeat the label—"hearing, hearing" rather than simply "hearing." The repetition can help when the mind resists coming back to the breath.

Try not to follow the movements of your mind; as soon as you realize where it has gone, label the distraction and come back to the breath. Sometimes you may notice immediately when your attention strays from the breath; other times you will find yourself in the midst of a story line in your head and realize that you've been distracted for some period of time. Don't worry about it—as soon as you realize you are not focused on your breath, label it and come back to the breath. Try to avoid the temptation—which can be quite strong—to continue following the story line. You can easily find yourself thinking, "I'll just finish thinking this thought and then I'll come back to the breath."

Don't chastise yourself for wandering. Simply make the mental note without evaluating or judging where your mind wandered or that it did so. If you do find yourself judging, make a mental note of the judgment (because that is where your mind was focused) and then gently return to the breath.

In the beginning, it will feel as though your mind is wandering constantly. You may feel as if you spend more time making mental notes than focusing on your breath. You are not alone; most people have this experience. There is nothing like meditation to make us realize exactly how unruly our minds are. Be patient. Over time greater concentration will develop and you will find that you can keep your attention on your breath for longer and longer periods.

When I first began to engage in this meditation, I had the mistaken idea that I could actively try to keep thoughts from rising. However, I quickly learned that we can't *try* to not think. I remember complaining to my meditation instructor that I was frustrated that I couldn't stop myself from thinking. His response was one of those things that seems completely obvious as soon as you hear it: Trying not to think is like trying to get rid of the ripples on a pool of water by smoothing them out with your hand. Just as the action of the hand inevitably creates more ripples in the water, trying not to think creates more mental activity, not less. The goal is simply to allow the object of your distraction to fade away, without actively doing anything to push it away. The instruction is always the same: make a mental note of where your mind has gone and then gently bring yourself back to the breath.

Remember to pay attention to what distracts you, however. If a particular "distraction" keeps surfacing, it is likely a sign of something significant you need to look at. The more we meditate, the more "stuff" that usually stays safely buried will come to the surface. Meditation forces us to look at things we are generally champions at avoiding. I'm not suggesting that you stop your shamatha practice and immediately sit with the issue that arises. Simply recognize it as something requiring your attention and set it aside with the intention of returning to it at a later point.

Application

I often find this shamatha practice a useful one with which to begin my prayer. If, for example, you are taking a break for prayer in the middle of your workday, a breathing meditation is a helpful way to transition from whatever you were doing before you turn to your prayer. Five minutes or so of focusing on the breath helps develop concentration for the rest of your prayer period. After you have been doing the practice for a while, you may not even need five minutes—simply bringing your focus to your breath for several breaths may be sufficient to "clear your mind" a bit. Once you become accustomed to the practice, you will find it can be helpful in any stressful situation. Even a few moments of focus on the breath can help make you feel better able to deal with the situation, by opening some space in the mind. In my third month of a long vipassana retreat in Thailand, I had to leave the retreat house and travel a few hours by bus to Bangkok to renew my visa. I went from the tranquility of the retreat grounds to the middle of the modern city. When I found myself almost disoriented by the hustle and bustle that assaulted all of my senses, I would focus on my breathing for a few moments, after which everything seemed calmer and more manageable. You will also find that if you engage in this practice on a regular basis—even for as little as fifteen minutes a day—your concentration will be greatly improved, even when you are not engaged in meditation.

There are various ways you can use the focus on the breath. One suggestion is to start a session by engaging in a visualization, as in some of the meditations in Part III. As you inhale, visualize the breath coming in as white light, and as you exhale, visualize the breath going out as black smoke. As you inhale the white light, visualize yourself absorbing good qualities of love, patience, and so on. As you exhale the black smoke, visualize yourself exhaling all of your worry, anxiety, and pain. If you are feeling depressed, the recommendation is to do this for ten minutes at the beginning of a prayer session.

Another suggestion is to recite short lines of prayer in rhythm with the breath, as you would recite the Jesus prayer. Thich Nhat Hanh suggests the following short exercise:

> Breathing in, I calm my body.
> Breathing out, I smile.
> Dwelling in the present moment,
> I know this is a wonderful moment.[3]

Repeat those four lines over and over, as long as you like.

Of the first line, Hanh says, "When I breathe in and recite this line, I actually experience my breathing calming my body and my mind." That relaxation continues into wonder as we breathe out, with a smile. The third line helps us recognize that we are here, right now, in this present moment. We exhale, knowing that this moment that we are in is a wonderful one.

Try it that way, or in a simplified way Hanh also suggests. As you breathe in, simply say to yourself, "Calming." As you exhale, say, "Smiling." With the next inhalation, say, "Present moment." With the exhalation, "Wonderful moment." Again, simply repeat these four lines over and over, in rhythm with your inhalations and exhalations.

Here is another variation. This comes from a prayer card I received from a retreat director at the end of an eight-day

Ignatian directed retreat. I haven't been able to discover the source of this prayer. Again, you want to recite the words in rhythm with your breathing, reciting the first two lines of each stanza as you inhale and the third and fourth lines as you exhale. You can repeat a single stanza for several rounds of inhalations and exhalations, or pray through the four stanzas one time each and then repeat the series when you are done, as many times as you wish. As in the first exercise, the idea is not to engage in deep analysis of the words, but simply to allow them to wash over you, allowing your whole being to express your desire for oneness with God.

O Holy One
down deep in my heart
enable me to join You
down deep in my heart.

O Holy One
down deep in my heart
enable me to know You
down deep in my heart.

O Holy One
down deep in my heart
enable me to love You
down deep in my heart.

O Holy One
down deep in my heart
enable me to follow You
down deep in my heart.

You can adapt this practice for use with any other simple prayer. If you have a favorite prayer, try praying it to the rhythm of your breath.

VIPASSANA

Basic Instruction

Vipassana meditation, also referred to as insight meditation or mindfulness meditation, is a common form of Theravadan Buddhist meditation. "Insight" here refers to insight into the true nature of reality. It is not a Tibetan Buddhist practice, but I include it here because I have practiced it extensively—once in a retreat in Thailand that lasted almost four months—and continue to find it a useful form of breathing meditation.

A comprehensive instruction in vipassana meditation is beyond the scope of this book. For those interested in learning more about this form of meditation, I recommend *Christian Insight Meditation: Following in the Footsteps of John of the Cross* by Meadow, Culligan, and Chowning, or *Insight Meditation: A Step-by-Step Course in How to Meditate*, by Sharon Salzberg and Joseph Goldstein.

Vipassana meditation begins with a focus on the breath as a way to calm the mind and develop concentration. Ultimately, the object of meditation is broadened to take in mindful observation, not only of the breath, but of sensations, feelings, and thoughts. Because the meditation requires both mindfulness and concentration, vipassana retreats typically involve alternating periods of sitting and walking meditation from morning to night. During such retreats, which vary in length from several days to several months, it is typical (at least in some retreat centers in

Thailand, but not always in the United States) to meet daily with an instructor, who listens to the retreatant's experience of the previous day, discusses it, and makes modifications in the balance of time between sitting and walking in order to keep a proper balance between mindfulness and concentration.

For personal practice outside of a retreat setting, I recommend that, as in shamatha meditation, you find a comfortable position that you can hold without feeling the need to make frequent adjustments. Place your hands one on top of the other on your lap, palms upward.

Once you are comfortably seated, focus on the movement of your abdomen as you breathe—on its expansion as you take in breath and its contraction as you exhale. At the end of your inhalation, make a mental note, "rising." At the end of your exhalation, make a mental note, "falling." You are merely observing here; the idea is neither to effect any change in how you breathe nor to analyze the process. Merely observe and label.

As with the shamatha process, when your mind wanders, simply bring it back. Label where your mind went—"hearing," "itching," "thinking." Label and return to the rising and falling of the inhalation and exhalation.

The first few times you do this practice, you should go no further than this. If you continue with it, you can start to add other objects of concentration as the breathing naturally slows and more space is present in between breaths. The next object to add is an awareness of the sitting posture. In the space between one exhalation and the next inhalation, allow the mind to be aware of the sense or feeling of the posture (a much more subtle object of awareness than the breath). So the rhythm becomes rising...falling...sitting. After some period of time, add a fourth object: the feeling of your hands touching each other. At this point, the rhythm becomes rising...falling...

sitting...touching. In advanced practice, the awareness can move beyond those four objects to take in thoughts, feelings, and other mental activities, but unless you are doing the practice in a retreat setting, keeping the focus on these four objects is sufficient.

Application

In Theravadan practice, this meditation is more than a means of developing mindfulness; it is seen as a way to gain a deeper understanding of the basic Buddhist truths of suffering, impermanence, and emptiness.

For Christians, vipassana has many potential benefits. Used at the beginning of a prayer session, it helps develop concentration and promotes a deeper experience of the analytical meditations or other subject matter of that prayer session. And once you are acquainted with the practice, it offers relief from stress just as shamatha does.

As a stand-alone practice, vipassana is extremely useful for the development of mindfulness, something that is as important for Christians as for Buddhists. Thich Nhat Hanh writes, "When we are mindful, touching deeply the present moment, we can see and listen deeply, and the fruits are always understanding, acceptance, love, and the desire to relieve suffering and bring joy.... To me, mindfulness is very much like the Holy Spirit."[4]

Vipassana also offers an opportunity to recognize that reactions are not automatic, that we can control our reactions to things. B. Alan Wallace describes mindfulness meditation as helping us to recognize "the spark before the flame,"[5] allowing us to make better choices about what conditions we act on and which ones we simply let go. In Viktor Frankl's words, it helps us see that "between stimulus and response, there is a space. In that space is our power to choose our response."[6] Engaging in vipassana practice does not guarantee that unwelcome states like anxiety will no longer arise. They will, some habitually. However, the fruit of sustained vipassana practice is that when such states arise, it is easier to see them as something that rises and then vanishes.

This effect of vipassana reminds me of my experience when I am given nitrous oxide before a painful dental procedure. The drug does not take the pain away. Rather, it seems to put a distance between me and the pain; I experience pain, but not as something I am involved in or that bothers me. Similarly, the meditation changes our reaction—certain states may continue to rise, but the meditation allows them to vanish without our getting caught up in them. Thus, the meditation can do a great deal to lessen the stress and anxiety of our lives. In fact, a recently reported study found that participants who engaged in mindfulness meditation showed structural changes in gray matter in the region of the brain connected with anxiety and stress.[7]

BRIEF NOTE ABOUT NON-BREATH-CENTERED MEANS OF STABILIZATION

Both shamatha and vipassana use the breath as an object of focus for developing concentration. Other objects can perform the same function.

Mantra recitation is a common Buddhist practice, and there are any number of mantras that are recited over and over as part of various prayer practices. While the mantras have meaning, they also help center the mind, allowing visualizations or other prayer activity to take place in a more concentrated manner. Many Tibetan Buddhist practices involve repeating a given mantra a specified number of times, and a *mala* (a set of prayer beads) is used to keep track of the number.

For Catholics, the Rosary performs the same function as mantra recitation. Praying the Rosary involves the repetition of a well-known prayer—the Hail Mary—to stabilize the mind as we engage in prayerful meditation. Pope John Paul II emphasized that the Rosary is not simply a matter of reciting a lot of words, but of providing a quiet rhythm and a lingering pace to allow us to meditate on the central events of the incarnation, life, death, and resurrection of Jesus. The repetition of this familiar prayer frees our mind to reflect on these events, to consider how they are lived out in the world, and to discern how we are called to respond. The physical act of holding beads while praying also helps us to concentrate. It anchors and centers us. The parallel to Buddhist practice is striking.

Chapter 21

Other Practices

A number of other Tibetan Buddhist practices are easily adaptable by Christians seeking to enrich their prayer lives. Many of them offer ways of disposing ourselves to God, of preparing our minds and opening our hearts to God. I present three such practices here.

PRECEPTS

Thich Nhat Hanh says that Buddhist precepts (or vows), like Judeo-Christian commandments, are "important jewels that we need to study and practice. They provide guidelines that can help us transform our suffering. Looking deeply at these precepts and commandments, we can learn the art of living in beauty."[1]

Buddhists believe that moral behavior disposes us to prayer, and the taking of precepts is seen as an important adjunct to meditation practice. In addition, taking vows is also seen as an acknowledgment of our responsibility for the happiness of others. Lama Thubten Zopa Rinpoche stressed the "incredible protection" we give to other beings by taking vows, suggesting that "the more you take vows, so much less harm other sentient beings receive from you."

All who follow a Buddhist path take vows to follow the five major precepts; they promise to refrain from killing, stealing, sexual misconduct, false speech, and alcohol and drug use. Anyone who considers himself or herself a serious Buddhist practitioner vows to live in accordance with these precepts. (The fifth is interpreted by many to entail using alcohol in moderation, rather than abstaining completely.)

There are also lifelong precepts or vows taken by Buddhist monks and nuns, similar to, but more numerous than, vows taken by Catholic priests and nuns.

On certain holidays and other special days, Tibetan Buddhist practitioners commit to follow the Eight Mahayana Precepts for a period of twenty-four hours, typically from sunrise to sunrise. In addition to a reaffirmation of the basic five vows, the Eight Mahayana Precepts add a vow to eat no more than one meal during the twenty-four-hour period, a vow to avoid acts that signify pride such as sitting on a high or ornate seat, and a vow to refrain from wearing jewelry, perfume, and other adornments and to forswear singing, dancing, and playing music. Breaking a precept is a serious matter and a person who does so is expected to perform some act of purification. Vows should not be taken lightly.

What is of interest here is not the specific content of the Eight Mahayana Precepts but the idea of making an intentional commitment to live in articulated vows for a period of time. This strikes me as a powerful practice for two reasons. There is a value to the mindfulness created by an affirmative act of taking a vow, even if obeying it presents no difficulty. It causes us to reflect on our reasons for taking a particular vow and what values the vow supports, potentially affecting our behavior in a positive way beyond the "letter of the law." For example, our (implicit) vow to live our lives in conformity with the Ten Commandments means we vow not to kill or steal. Taking a vow against killing and stealing in an intentional way may encourage us to be more loving or more generous.

Second, we know that there are certain behaviors, thought patterns, and tendencies we would do well rid ourselves of. For some it may be a sharp tongue. For others it may be a "me first" tendency. There may be some things that we don't like to admit to, but wish we could abandon.

We recognize that such behaviors, thought patterns, and tendencies are inimical to our spiritual growth, but they are hard to eradicate. Promising, "I will never, ever again do..." is difficult. The beauty of the twenty-four-hour vow is that, while it seems difficult or impossible to reform some behavior every day for the rest of our lives, there is little that is too hard to commit to for a single day. This is precisely the understanding that underlies the slogan "Just for today," well known to Alcoholics Anonymous and Narcotics Anonymous members, whose recovery is based on a "one day at a time" approach. The first part of the Twelve-Step *Just for Today* meditation reflects that well: "Just for today, I will try to live through this day only, and not tackle my whole life problem at once. I can do something for twelve hours that would appall me if I felt that I had to keep it up for a lifetime."

A Christian could simply affirmatively commit to live in the Ten Commandments or the Beatitudes in a full and mindful way for twenty-four hours. You could, however, profitably look to your own life and consider what things you most want to change. What might it be helpful for you to intentionally vow to refrain from for a twenty-four-hour period? You can determine the content of your vows based on a prayerful determination of what will be most beneficial to your spiritual growth. If you use the Commandments or the Beatitudes, try to formulate the vow in a way that is personally meaningful to you. Don't merely vow that "for twenty-four hours I will practice poverty of spirit," but give content to it that will make it more concrete for you. Spend some time reflecting on what it means in the context of your life to be poor in spirit, and frame the vow in those terms. That might take the form, for example, of a vow to affirmatively call to mind your dependence on God's grace before tackling a difficult task.

If the practice appeals to you, you can lengthen the period for which you maintain your promise. But be careful not to promise more than you are comfortable with. If you decide to make a promise lasting more than twenty-four hours, you may find it helpful to put it in writing, and place it somewhere where you will notice it and be mindful of it. On a Tibetan Buddhist website I once saw a "commitment card" on which practitioners were to write down a new practice they were vowing to keep. The card took the form of a letter to the practitioner's guru that acknowledged respect and devotion to the guru and left space for the signer to fill in the promise and the length of time the promise would be kept. You could do something similar with written prayer to Jesus that records your commitment.

Following is one suggestion for a twenty-four-hour set of precepts based on the Ten Commandments. You may or may not wish to try it in this form, but it can serve as a model for creating a practice that works for you. There is no "right" or "wrong" way to do it so long as you are sincere in trying to live purely in the vow or vows you promise to keep.

One Suggested Practice

Taking the Vows

Visualize Jesus in the space in front of you. As you gaze on his face, develop the strong desire to be one with him and his Father. Now pray:

So that I may grow in union with my God, and for the benefit of all of God's creatures, I [your name] will live this twenty-four-hour period in accordance with the following vows:
I will give time to God in prayer this day.

I will not use God's name lightly or carelessly this day.

I will do some special act of kindness for my parents [or children or spouse] this day.

I will not harbor anger or hatred toward another in my heart this day.

I will be chaste in my thoughts, words, and deeds this day.

I will take nothing that is not mine this day and I will make an effort to share with another something that is mine.

I will not gossip about anyone this day or say anything that will cause division or hatred in others.

If the qualities or possessions of another person arouse jealous or envious thoughts in me today, I will let them vanish without grasping them.

Lord, help me purely keep these vows, which I commit to for this twenty-four-hour period, so that I may grow in you. By the actions I commit and those I refrain from, may others grow closer to you. Amen.

Prayer at the End of the Twenty-Four-Hour Period

At the end of the period of your vows, take stock. Start by recognizing that you are in God's presence and ask for God's grace to honestly assess your success at adhering to the vows you promised to keep.

Look back over the day, thinking of each vow one by one. Are there places you felt you did a particularly good job of keeping to the vows? Are there places where, in retrospect, you could have done a better job?

Take both before God. Offer up those areas where you feel you lived up to what you promised, hearing God say to you, "Well done, my good and faithful servant." Then look with God at those areas where you didn't do as well, asking God for what you need to be able to adhere more closely to that particular vow. Then speak whatever words of thanksgiving and praise come to you. And be sure to give God time to communicate with you that which God desires to tell you.

SEVEN-LIMB PRACTICE / MANDALA OFFERING

A Tibetan practice that I always loved is the Seven-Limb Practice. The instruction is to visualize your root teacher in the space before you, and reflect on his qualities. Then you offer this prayer, with appropriate visualizations and reflections at each line. The actual words of the prayer as I was taught it are in italics, followed by an explanation of what accompanies the recitation:

Reverently, I prostrate with my body, speech, and mind
    While reciting these words, one can perform a physical prostration—a formal prostration on hands and knees or a simple bow with hands folded at the heart—or visualize making a prostration. One prostrates with body, speech, and mind, which means the physical act is accompanied by recitation of the prayer with a respectful and focused mind.

And present clouds of every type of offerings, actual and imagined.
    Here one cultivates a vision of offering to the teacher all varieties of pleasant offerings—food, drink, flowers, lights, incense, precious gems. Everything offered is imagined as purely and wonderfully as the imagination is capable of making it.

I declare all my negative actions accumulated since beginningless time,
    This step involves identifying and acknowledging one's weaknesses, with the desire to be purified of their negative

effects and the resolve never to commit unvirtuous actions in the future.

And rejoice in the merit of all the Holy and ordinary beings.

Rejoicing is considered a great practice. Cultivating a mind that rejoices in the good qualities and happiness of others serves to counter feelings of jealousy. The instruction is to reflect on the qualities and deeds of one's guru, as rejoicing in the virtue of holy beings is thought to create extensive merit, as well as "ordinary" people whose qualities and deeds one is aware of.

Please remain until samsara ends
And turn the Wheel of Dharma for sentient beings.
I dedicate the merit created by myself and others to the great Enlightenment.

The final petitions plead for long life for the guru and that the guru continue to give teachings. The prayer ends with a dedication of merits, a common ending of Buddhist prayers.

The step I always found particularly powerful is the second— offering. Tibetans have an entire practice, the Mandala Offering, that is an extended offering to the Buddhas and to the teachers of the person making the offering. The point is to offer everything— the entire universe—including all of the things you possess and even those things you do not possess. The aim of the prayer is to be free from attachments and possessiveness, all of the things that hinder us from achieving deep realizations.

Many Christians engage in some prayer of self-offering, whether daily or occasionally. For example, every day, my own prayer includes recitation of St. Ignatius's Suscipe:

Take Lord, and receive all my liberty, my memory, my under-
standing, and my entire will, all that I have and call my own. You

have given it all to me. To you, Lord, I return it. Everything is
yours; do with it what you will. Give me only your love and your
grace. That is enough for me.[2]

Others use the self-offering prayer of St. Therese of Lisieux:

In order to live in an act of perfect love, I offer myself as a victim of
holocaust to your Merciful Love, imploring you to consume me
unceasingly and to let overflow into my soul the floods of infinite
tenderness contained in you, that thus I may become a martyr to
your love, O my God....May this martyrdom, after having pre-
pared me to appear before you, allow me to die at last, and may my
soul without delay leap into the eternal embrace of your Merciful
Love. O my Beloved, with every beat of my heart I want to renew
this offering an infinite number of times until the shadows of
night, having been dispelled, I can tell you of my love face-to-face
for all eternity.[3]

Others favor this prayer of Charles de Foucauld:

Father, I abandon myself into your hands; do with me what you
will. Whatever you may do, I thank you: I am ready for all, I accept
all. Let only your will be done in me, and in all your creatures—I
wish no more than this, O Lord.

Into your hands I commend my soul; I offer it to you with all the
love of my heart, for I love you, Lord, and so need to give myself, to
surrender myself into your hands, without reserve, and with bound-
less confidence, for you are my Father.[4]

There are many other Christian prayers of self-offering. If you
already have a favorite, I am not suggesting that you replace it
with the Tibetan one. But I hope that a glimpse of the Tibetan

Seven-Limb and Mandala practices might enrich your prayer by encouraging you to add some visualization to the process.

There is a danger when we recite a prayer very frequently that it becomes rote; we find ourselves quickly running through the words, our attention half on the words of the prayer and half someplace else. If we take each phrase of our self-offering and savor it, allowing our minds to give some visual content to what we are saying, our prayer becomes deeper.

If a prayer of self-offering is not already part of your practice, the elements of the Tibetan practice offer a nice rubric for the creation of one. The steps of the prayer, refuge and prostration, offering, reconciliation, rejoicing, requests for teacher, and dedication, easily form part of a Christian prayer. In place of visualizing a root teacher, as a Buddhist would do, you visualize Christ standing before you.

In neither the Tibetan nor the Christian form of offering is the idea that we are giving something Buddha or God needs. Buddhists view the purpose of the offering as the accumulation of merit and development of detachment from physical possessions. The practice is seen as a direct opposing force to avarice and covetousness. For Christians, as the Suscipe prayer suggests, the idea is not so different. It is to place God first in our lives, letting go of attachments that usurp God's place at the center of our lives.

AWARENESS OF CONSCIOUSNESS

Buddhists speak of the nature of the mind as clear and knowing, as having the qualities of luminosity and awareness. The delusions from which we suffer do not penetrate to the essence or nature of the mind, and thus can be rooted out. It is sometimes said that the mind is like the sky and delusions are the clouds. Another analogy sees the mind as clear water and delusions as the mud that clouds it. The distinction is important: if the delusions were one with the mind, they could not be dispelled. Lama Thubten Zopa Rinpoche often used the image of a mirror and dirt: if the dirt was one with the mirror, the dirt could not be cleared away; you cannot clean dirt from dirt. But because the two are distinct the dirt can be cleared away. From a Buddhist perspective the goal of spiritual practice is to clear away delusions so that the mind can rest in its natural state.

The final Tibetan Buddhist practice I will introduce is designed to help us get in touch with the nature of mind itself. It may be described as a bare awareness of consciousness. I choose to end with it because it is already part of the Christian contemplative tradition, highlighting again as I come to a close the many areas of congruence between the two traditions.

St. Gregory Palamas encouraged monastics to lead "a life of self-attentiveness and stillness to bring their intellect back and to enclose it within their body, and particularly within that inner-most body within the body that we call the heart."[5] St. Theophan the Recluse observed that "images, however sacred they may be, retain the attention outside, whereas at the time of prayer the attention must be within—in the heart. The concentration of attention in the heart—that is the starting point of prayer."[6] B. Alan Wallace writes that "Christian contemplatives through the ages have reported exceptional states of inner knowledge and genuine well-being—a kind of 'truth-given joy'—that arise when the heart is purified and brought to rest in its own innermost depths."[7] Lay Christians in the West seem to be mostly unaware of this practice in their own tradition.

The practice of Christian contemplatives is similar to the Tibetan practice. Note the similarities between descriptions from a Tibetan teacher and a Christian one.

Buddhist instruction:

Sit upon a soft cushion in a solitary, darkened room. Vacantly direct your eyes into the intervening space in front of you. Completely dispense with all thoughts pertaining to the past, future, and present, as well as wholesome, unwholesome, and ethically neutral thoughts.... Bring no thoughts to mind. Let the mind, like a cloudless sky, be clear, empty and evenly free of grasping, and settle your awareness in a state of utter vacuity. By so doing, you will experience a quiescent state of awareness imbued with joy, luminosity, and nonconceptuality. Within that state, note whether you experience any attachment, hatred, clinging, grasping, laxity, or excitation, and recognize the difference between virtues and vices.[8]

Christian instruction:

Shift your awareness from the distraction to the awareness itself, to the aware-ing. There is nothing but this same luminous vastness, this depthless depth. What gazes into luminous vastness is itself luminous vastness. There is not a separate self who is afraid or angry or jealous. Clearly fear, anger, jealousy may be present, but we won't find anyone who is afraid, angry, jealous, etc., just luminous, depthless depth gazing into luminous, depthless depth.[9]

We might call this "depthless depth" the substrate of the mind or the substrate consciousness. B. Alan Wallace likens the mind in its natural state to "a luminously transparent snow globe in which all the agitated particles of mental activities have come to rest."[10]

As with everything I have presented here, my invitation is that you try the practice. The instruction is simple, since all we are trying to do is to rest our consciousness clearly and continuously on itself. Simply let your heart acquire stillness. Let your awareness rest on itself. Don't try to form any images. Don't try to do anything. You are simply letting all of the activities of your mind go.

The practice has powerful benefits. First, it helps us realize at a deep level that we are not our thoughts or our feelings. Martin Laird writes,

> The marvelous world of thoughts, sensation, emotions, and inspiration, the spectacular world of creation around us, are all patterns of stunning weather on the holy mountain of God. But we are not the weather.... When the mind is brought to stillness we see that we are the mountain and not the changing patterns of weather appearing on the mountain.... For a lifetime we have taken this weather—our thoughts and feelings—to be ourselves, taken ourselves to be this video to which the attention is riveted. Stillness reveals that we are the silent, vast awareness in which the video is played. To glimpse this fundamental truth is to be liberated.[11]

Second, there is a freedom in realizing that our minds are spacious, and not the cramped spaces they sometimes appear to be. Laird talks about the fact that the "mental cage in which we live much of our lives... makes us believe we are separate from God."[12] The practice helps us sink into the ground of our being, overcoming the sense of separation.

If you engage in this practice with any regularity, you are likely to find, as described by Hesychios the Priest, that when your "heart has acquired stillness, it will perceive the heights and depths of knowledge; and the ear of the still intellect will be made to hear marvelous things from God."[13] Why not try it?

Conclusion

Prayer is an essential element of our lives as Christians. We cannot grow in our relationship with God unless we take time to nurture that relationship through prayer. That means not only the quick prayers we may offer up as we are driving to work or doing the dishes. It also means making the time to sit quietly with God and giving God a chance to communicate with us.

How we pray is much less important than that we pray. Nonetheless, we can all benefit from learning to pray in new ways. My own Christian prayer life has been greatly enriched by incorporating elements of meditations I practiced during my years as a Buddhist. I pray that the same will be true for you and that these meditations become a source of nourishment for you on your spiritual journey.

The ultimate goal of any book of spirituality is to help readers deepen their commitment to their faith and enable them to walk more fully in the light of God's truth. There are significant differences between Buddhism and Christianity, but the two faiths share many values. It is my hope that reflecting on these shared values and as well as on the differences between the two faiths will help deepen your understanding of Christianity and strengthen your life as a disciple of Christ.

Perhaps you've been praying with some of the meditations as you've been reading. If you have, I hope you will continue to do so. They will become easier and more natural the more you practice them.

Or it may be that you've read as far as this conclusion without having seriously tried any of the meditations, perhaps because you haven't found the uninterrupted time to do so or because the prospect of getting started has seemed a bit overwhelming. I urge you to find the time to give it a chance. Pick one meditation, the one that attracted you the most, and start there. Once you do, it will start to feel much less overwhelming and you will be encouraged to try others. Remember that the only way you can evaluate a practice is to test it by your own experience. So give it a try!

Blessings on your spiritual journey!

ACKNOWLEDGMENTS

It is hard to know where to begin to acknowledge those who had a hand, directly or indirectly, in my ability to write this book.

To those who were my teachers during my years as a Buddhist, I have tremendous love and gratitude both for what I learned about Buddhist practice and for the development of my sense of spirituality. Foremost among them are Lama Thubten Zopa Rinpoche, who was my root teacher during those years, His Holiness the Dalai Lama, one of the holiest persons I have ever met, and Jitamaro Bikkhu, who gave me my first instruction in vipassana meditation in Thailand and directed me during each of my vipassana retreats there.

I am equally indebted to those who aided my spiritual growth following my return to Catholicism, most especially John Freund, C.M., who has helped me retain a breadth of vision that continually deepens my understanding of my faith and who also read portions of the manuscript for me, and Joe Costantino, S.J., and Karen Doyle, S.S.J., who oversaw and participated in my training in Ignatian spirituality and retreat house ministry. Each of these dear friends and mentors encouraged me in this project.

I am grateful for comments on the early chapters of the book from my friend and colleague Chato Hazelbaker and to several people who used and gave me feedback on the meditations in Part III: Austin Caster (who also provided valuable research assistance for me), Susan Martin, and George Christopher. Cynthia Read, my editor at Oxford, provided invaluable editing of the book. Whenever I think of her contributions, I send a prayer of thanksgiving for my friend Randy Buck, who was the person who introduced me to Cynthia.

To the University of St. Thomas School of Law I am indebted for a research leave that allowed me time to concentrate on the book. I am also grateful to the sisters at St. Benedict's Monastery in St. Joseph, Minnesota, who warmly welcomed me into their community during several stays with them as part of the monastery's Visiting Scholars Program. My thanks also to Bethany Fletcher, Deborah Hackerson, and Kelli Riley for proofreading and other technical assistance in connection with preparation of the manuscript.

Last, but not least, my husband and daughter, Dave and Elena, provide me with constant support and encouragement in all that I do. To all those I have named here, and those I have inadvertently neglected to mention, I am enormously grateful.

GLOSSARY OF BUDDHIST TERMS

analytical meditation A form of Tibetan Buddhist meditation that engages the faculties of intellect and imagination as the means of allowing one to come to deep realizations about fundamental truths.

bodhicitta The determination or aspiration to attain enlightenment for the sake of all sentient beings; a mind that cherishes others over the self.

bodhisattva A being who has fully attained a mind of bodhicitta and whose sole motivation is to benefit others.

cyclic existence Continuous cycle of birth and death that one undergoes until reaching Enlightenment.

dependent arising A term that refers to the fact that all things exist in dependence on causes and conditions, that nothing exists inherently or independently.

Dharma Teachings of the Buddha; Buddhist doctrine.

Eight Worldly Concerns The worldly concerns that tend to motivate the actions of ordinary humans.

emptiness The lack of inherent, independent existence of all things.

equanimity A state of lacking attachment or aversion.

guru Spiritual teacher.

Hinayana One of the traditions of Buddhist thought; referred to by Mahayana Buddhists as the smaller vehicle.

karma The law of cause and effect: virtuous actions lead to happiness and nonvirtuous acts lead to suffering.

Lam-Rim A shorthand reference to the *Lam-Rim Chen Mo*, a set of practices offering a graduated path to enlightenment.

lama The Tibetan word for guru; a spiritual teacher.

lo-jong Tibetan thought transformation teachings.

Mahayana The spiritual path of those who seek enlightenment for the sake of bringing others to enlightenment.

mandala A practice in which everything in the universe is offered to the Buddhas and to one's teachers.

mantra A sound, word, or group of words repeatedly recited or sung with the intent of transforming the mind.

mindfulness A state of calm awareness; mindfulness meditation practice aims to keep one in the present moment, aware of what is transpiring in the now.

nonduality The idea that all existing phenomena are by nature beyond duality, that things that appear to be independent or distinct are really not separate things.

prostration A Buddhist practice that shows reverence by lowering the body to the floor; in a full prostration, one is in a fully prone position on the floor.

refuge In Buddhist terms, reliance on the Buddha, Dharma, and Sangha for guidance on the spiritual path.

renunciation The state of mind of not being attached to worldly pleasures or having aversion to unpleasant worldly situations.

root delusions Ignorance, attachment, and anger; the three wrong thoughts that create suffering, from which all other delusions flow.

samsara The state of continually taking rebirth under the control of karma and delusions.

sangha Refers to those who have realized emptiness when used to refer to the third object of refuge; the term is also used to refer to ordained monks and nuns.

Sanskrit The language of many original Buddhist texts.

sentient being Refers to all beings in any of the six realms of samsara, who are subject to the law of cause and effect; all beings who have not yet attained enlightenment.

shamatha A form of stabilization or concentrative meditation, aimed at calming the mind and helping one develop the ability to focus the mind single-pointedly on an object until the mind can rest on the object for a significant period of time.

shunyata The correct view of emptiness.

sutra A scriptural Buddhist text and its teachings and practices.

tantra A form of teaching that is considered to offer a quicker path to enlightenment than by following the path of the sutra; often referred to as the esoteric teachings of the Buddha.

Therevada One of the oldest schools of Buddhism, it is the form of Buddhism most commonly found in Southeast Asia.

tong-len Literally, giving and taking; refers to a meditation technique in which one takes upon oneself the suffering of others and gives over to them what they need to relieve them of their suffering.

vipassana One of the oldest Buddhist forms of meditation, its aim is to see things the way they really are through a practice of deepened mindfulness; sometimes also called insight meditation.

SUGGESTIONS FOR FURTHER READING

Buddhism and Christianity

Borg, Marcus, ed. *Jesus and Buddha: The Parallel Sayings*. Berkeley, CA: Ulysses Press, 2004.

Chetwynd, Tom. *Zen and the Kingdom of Heaven: Reflections on the Tradition of Meditation in Christianity and Zen Buddhism*. Boston: Wisdom Publications, 2001.

Dalai Lama, His Holiness the. *The Good Heart: A Buddhist Perspective on the Teachings of Jesus*. Boston: Wisdom Publications, 1996.

Kasimow, Harold, John Keenan, and Linda Klepinger Keenan, eds. *Beside Still Waters: Jews, Christians, and the Way of the Buddha*. Boston: Wisdom Publications, 2003.

Knitter, Paul F. *Without Buddha I Could Not Be a Christian*. Oxford: OneWorld Publications, 2009.

Meadow, Mary Jo. *Gentling the Heart: Buddhist Loving-Kindness Practice for Christians*. New York: Crossroad, 1994.

Meadow, Mary Jo, Kevin Culligan, and Daniel Chowning. *Christian Insight Meditation: Following in the Footsteps of John of the Cross*. Boston: Wisdom Publications, 2007.

Nhat Hanh, Thich. *Going Home: Jesus and Buddha as Brothers*. New York: Riverhead Books, 1999.

Suzuki, Daisetz Teitaro. *Mysticism: Christian and Buddhist*. London: Routledge Classics, 2002.

Wallace, B. Alan. *Mind in the Balance: Meditation in Science, Buddhism, and Christianity*. New York: Columbia University Press, 2009.

Prayer, Mysticism, and Interspirituality

Dalai Lama, His Holiness the. *Toward a True Kinship of Faiths: How the World's Religions Can Come Together*. New York: Doubleday, 2010.
Rohr, Richard. *The Naked Now: Learning to See as the Mystics See*. New York: Crossroad, 2009.
Steindl-Rast, David. *Deeper Than Words: Living the Apostles' Creed*. New York: Image, 2010.
Teasdale, Wayne. *The Mystic Heart*. Novato, CA: New World Library, 1999.

Tibetan Buddhist Meditation

McDonald, Kathleen. *How to Meditate: A Practical Guide*. 2nd ed. Edited by Robina Courtin. Boston: Wisdom Publications, 2005.
Rabten, Geshe. *The Essential Nectar: Meditations on the Buddhist Path*. Boston: Wisdom Publications, 1984.

COPYRIGHT PERMISSION ACKNOWLEDGMENTS

I acknowledge permission of the copyright holders to quote from the following works:

Scripture quotations taken from the New American Standard Bible, Copyright 1960, 1962, 1963, 1968, 1971, 1972, 1973, 1975, 1977, 1995 by The Lockman Foundation. Used by permission. www.Lockman.org.

Lama Yeshe, excerpts from *Introduction to Tantra: A Vision of Totality.* Copyright © 1987 by Lama Zopa Rinpoche. Reprinted with the permission of The Permissions Company, Inc. on behalf of Wisdom Publications, www.wisdompubs.org.

Lama Zopa Rinpoche, excerpts from *Perfect Freedom: The Great Value of Being Human.* Copyright © 1995 by Lama Zopa Rinpoche. Reprinted with the permission of The Permissions Company, Inc. on behalf of Wisdom Publications, www.wisdompubs.org.

Lama Yeshe and Lama Zopa Rinpoche, excerpts from *Wisdom Energy: Basic Buddhist Teachings.* Copyright © 2000 by Lama Thubten Zopa Rinpoche. Reprinted with the permission of The Permissions Company, Inc. on behalf of Wisdom Publications, www.wisdompubs.org.

Kathleen McDonald, excerpts from *How to Meditate: A Practical Guide.* Copyright © 1984 by Wisdom Publications. Reprinted with the permission of The Permissions Company, Inc. on behalf of Wisdom Publications, www.wisdompubs.org.

His Holiness the Dalai Lama, excerpts from *The Good Heart: A Buddhist Perspective on the Teachings of Jesus,* translated by Geshe Thupten Jinpa.

NOTES

Introduction

1. Gerard Manley Hopkins, *Poems*, ed. Robert Seymour Bridges and William Henry Gardner (Oxford: Oxford University Press, 1948), 57.
2. Joseph Cardinal Ratzinger, Congregation of the Doctrine of the Faith, *Letter to the Bishops of the Catholic Church on Some Aspects of Christian Meditation*, par. 16 (October 15, 1989).

Chapter 1

1. Peter C. Phan, "Evangelization and Interreligious Dialogue: Compatible Parts of Christian Mission?" Lecture, Santa Clara University, Santa Clara, CA, February 23, 2010, 27.
2. Harold Kasimow, John P. Keenan, and Linda Klepinger Keenan, eds., *Beside Still Waters: Jews, Christians, and the Way of the Buddha* (Boston: Wisdom Publications, 2003), 15–16.
3. Alan Lew, "Becoming Who You Always Were: The Story of a Zen Rabbi," in Kasimow, Keenan, and Keenan, *Beside Still Waters*, 52, 59.
4. Tom Chetwynd, *Zen and the Kingdom of Heaven: Reflections on the Tradition of Meditation in Christianity and Zen Buddhism* (Boston: Wisdom Publications, 2001), 3.
5. Ibid., 39.

6. Thomas Merton, *Conjectures of a Guilty Bystander* (New York: Doubleday Image, 1966), 143–144.

7. Marcus Borg, ed., *Jesus and Buddha: The Parallel Sayings* (Berkeley, CA: Ulysses Press, 2004), 11.

8. Raimon Panikkar, *The Intrareligious Dialogue* (Mahwah, NJ: Paulist Press, 1999), 48.

9. John Stuart Mill, *Mill's "On Liberty"* (Millis, Angora Publications, 2003), 43.

10. Syliva Boorstein, "It's a No Karma Event," in Kasimow, Keenan, and Keenan, *Beside Still Waters*, 28.

11. Roger Corless, "A Form for Buddhist-Christian Coinherent Meditation," *Buddhist-Christian Studies* 14:139–144 (1994). In this article, Corless outlines a meditation practice aimed at allowing someone to acknowledge "Buddhism and Christianity as two Absolute Systems coinhering on the same plane (in humanity as a whole) and in your own consciousness" (139).

12. Paul F. Knitter, *Without Buddha I Could Not Be a Christian* (Oxford: OneWorld, 2009), 216.

13. *Catechism of the Catholic Church*, 2nd ed. (Washington, DC: United States Catholic Conference, 1994), 849.

14. *The Decree on Ecumenism*, http://www.vatican.va/roman_curia/pontifical_councils/chrstuni/card-kasper-docs/rc_pc_chrstuni_doc_20041111_kasper-ecumenism_en.html (2004), 23.

15. *Catechism*, 67, 86.

16. Congregation of the Doctrine of the Faith, *Declaration "Dominus Iesus" on the Unicity and Salvific Universality of the Jesus Christ and the Church*, http://www.vatican.va/roman_curia/congregations/cfaith/documents/rc_con_cfaith_doc_20000806_dominus-iesus_en.html (2000), sec. 20.

17. Paul VI, *Declaration on the Relation of the Church to Non-Christian Religions Nostra Aetate*, http://www.vatican.va/archive/hist_councils/ii_vatican_council/documents/vat-ii_decl_19651028_nostra-aetate_en.html (October 28, 1965), 2.

18. John Paul II, *Crossing the Threshold of Hope* (New York: Knopf, 1994), 147–149.

19. The letter is quoted in Phan, "Evangelization," 12.

20. His Holiness Tenzin Gyatso, The Fourteenth Dalai Lama, *A Human Approach to World Peace* (Boston: Wisdom Publications, 1984).

21. Nathan Katz, "From Jubu to Oj," in Kasimow, Keenan, and Keenan, *Beside Still Waters*, 37.

22. Ibid., 35.

23. Thich Nhat Hanh, *Interbeing: Fourteen Guidelines for Engaged Buddhism* (Berkeley, CA: Parallax Press, 1987), 87.

Chapter 2

1. Jack Kornfield, introduction to Borg, *Jesus and Buddha*, 6–7.
2. *Dominus Iesus*, par. 21.
3. His Holiness the Dalai Lama, *Toward a True Kinship of Faiths: How the World's Religions Can Come Together* (New York: Doubleday Religion, 2010), 110.
4. Pope Benedict XVI, *Prayer for the End of the Year: A Strange Thing Called Time*, December 31, 2009, pars. 2–3.
5. Rowan Williams, *Tokens of Trust* (Louisville, KY: Westminster John Knox Press, 2007), 36.
6. Lama Yeshe, *Introduction to Tantra: A Vision of Totality* (Boston: Wisdom Publications, 1987), 29.
7. Lama Thubten Zopa Rinpoche, *Perfect Freedom: The Great Value of Being Human*, rev. ed. (Boston: Wisdom Publications 1995), 9.
8. Merton, *Conjectures*, 48.
9. Yeshe, *Introduction to Tantra*, 23.
10. Congregation of the Doctrine of the Faith, *Christian Meditation*, par. 19.
11. Yeshe, *Introduction to Tantra*, 23–24.
12. Personal notes from teachings given by Lama Zopa Rinpoche during a Chenrezig Initiation on December 23, 1987, at Kopan Monastery.
13. Lama Thubten Zopa Rinpoche, *Transcript: Practicing the Good Heart* (Boston: Wisdom Publications, 1988), 2.
14. Dalai Lama, *Toward a True Kinship of Faiths*, 59, 57.
15. Kensur Losang Thubten Rinpoche, Teachings on Emptiness, Kopan Monastery, May 1988.
16. Zopa, *Practicing the Good Heart*, 1.
17. Udyoga Parva, *The Mahabharata*, book 5 of 18, trans. Sri Kisari Mohan Ganguli (Forgotten Books, 2008), 61.
18. Pope John Paul II, Address before Recitation of the Angelus at St. Peter's Square, June 15, 2003.
19. Richard W. Garnett, "Christian Witness, Moral Anthropology, and the Death Penalty," in *Religion and the Death Penalty: A Call for Reckoning*, ed. Eric C. Owen and Eric P. Elshtein (Grand Rapids, MI: Eerdmans, 2004), 154.
20. Adam Smith, *The Wealth of Nations*, Oxford World's Classics ed. (1776; repr. Oxford: Oxford University Press, 1998), 22.
21. Tenzin Gyatso, "The Fourteenth Dalai Lama, Compassion and the Individual: Our Need for Love," http://www.dalailama.com/messages/compassion.
22. Dalai Lama, *Toward a True Kinship*, 124.
23. Martin Buber, *Tales of the Hasidim* (New York: Schocken Books, 1991).

24. Lama Yeshe, *Universal Love: The Yoga Method of Buddha Maitreya* (Boston: Wisdom Publications, 2008), 114.
25. Dalai Lama, *Toward A True Kinship*, 9.
26. Chetwynd, *Zen*, 59.
27. B. Alan Wallace, *Mind in the Balance: Meditation in Science, Buddhism and Christianity* (New York: Columbia University Press, 2009), 85–86.
28. Richard Rohr, *The Naked Now: Learning to See as the Mystics See* (New York: Crossroad, 2009), 12.
29. Brother David Steindl-Rast, *Deeper Than Words: Living the Apostles' Creed* (New York: Doubleday Religion, 2010), 23.
30. Kevin Culligan, Mary Jo Meadows, and Daniel Chowning, Purifying the Heart: Buddhist Insight Meditation for Christians (New York: Crossroad, 1994) 35.
31. Yeshe, *Introduction to Tantra*, 36.
32. Carol Ludwig and Robert Gardenhire III, "Being Present to Each Other: An Interview with Ron Rolheiser, OMI," *Presence: An International Journal of Spiritual Direction* 15:6–12 (June 2009).

Chapter 3

1. Philip Zaleski and Carol Zaleski, *Prayer: A History* (New York: Houghton Mifflin, 2005), 4.
2. Rohr, *The Naked Now*, 23.
3. Hugo Enomiya-Lassalle, *Zen—Way to Enlightenment* (London: Burns & Oates, 1967), 77.
4. Merton, *Conjectures*, 156–158.
5. Ursula King, *Christian Mystics: Their Lives and Legacies throughout the Ages* (New York: HiddenSpring, 2001), 3.
6. Robert S. Ellwood, *Mysticism and Religion* (Upper Saddle River, NJ: Prentice-Hall, 1980), 35.
7. Roger Corless, *I Am Food: The Mass in Planetary Perspective* (New York: Crossroad, 1981), 33.
8. Kensur Losang Thubten Rinpoche, Four Noble Truths, notes from oral teaching given at Kopan Monastery in May 1988.
9. Lama Yeshe and Lama Zopa Rinpoche, *Wisdom Energy: Basic Buddhist Teachings*, 25th anniversary ed. (Boston: Wisdom Publications, 2000), 22.
10. Lama Yeshe, *Introduction to Tantra*, 35.
11. Jalal al din Rumi (Maulana), *The Sufi Path of Love: The Spiritual Teachings of Rumi*, trans. William C. Chittick (New York: SUNY Press, 1983), 8.
12. Congregation of the Doctrine of the Faith, *Christian Meditation*, par. 27.

13. Boorstein, "No-Karma Event," 28.
14. Deepak Chopra, *The Third Jesus: The Christ We Cannot Ignore* (New York: Harmony Books, 2008), 20.

Chapter 4

1. Congregation of the Doctrine of the Faith, *Christian Meditation*, par. 28.
2. *Dominus Iesus*, par. 21.
3. "Eruption of Truth: An Interview with Raimon Panikkar," *Christian Century*, August 16–23, 2000, 834.
4. Enomiya-Lassalle, *Zen—Way to Enlightenment*, 9.
5. Kathleen McDonald, *How to Meditate: A Practical Guide* (Boston: Wisdom Publications, 1984), 20.

PART III

1. McDonald, *How to Meditate*, 57.
2. His Holiness the Dalai Lama, *The Good Heart: A Buddhist Perspective on the Teachings of Jesus* (Boston: Wisdom Publications, 1996), 46–47.
3. Corless, *I Am Food*, 46.

Chapter 5

1. Dalai Lama, *The Good Heart*, 48.
2. Personal notes from teaching given by Lama Thubten Zopa Rinpoche on Emptiness during a meditation course at Kopan Monastery in 1983.

Chapter 6

1. Sogyal Rinpoche, *Glimpse after Glimpse: Daily Reflections on Living and Dying* (San Francisco: HarperCollins, 1995), 14.

Chapter 7

1. Geshe Rabten, *The Essential Nectar: Meditations on the Buddhist Path* (Boston: Wisdom Publications, 1984), 147.
2. Yeshe and Zopa, *Wisdom Energy*, 101.
3. Oscar Romero, *The Church's Mission*, sermon delivered on May 8, 1977.

Chapter 8

1. Personal notes from teaching of Lama Zopa Rinpoche, Kopan Monastery, December 1987.
2. Lama Zopa Rinpoche, *Perfect Freedom: The Great Value of Being Human* (Boston: Wisdom Publications, 1995), 2.

Chapter 9

1. Geshe Rabten, *The Essential Nectar*, 44.

Chapter 11

1. Santideva, *Bodhisattvacharyavatara: A Guide to the Bodhisattva's Way of Life* (Dharamsala, India: Library of Tibetan Works and Archives, 1979), 23–25.

Chapter 12

1. Yeshe and Zopa, *Wisdom Energy*, 72 (quoting Je Tsongkhapa).
2. Ibid., 74.

Chapter 14

1. Lama Yeshe, "Dissolution," in *Wisdom Energy 2* (Boston: Wisdom Publications, 1979), 36.
2. Personal notes from teachings given by Lama Zopa Rinpoche during a Chenrezig Initiation, December 23, 1987.
3. Geshe Rabten, *The Essential Nectar*, 85.
4. Personal notes from teachings given by Lama Zopa Rinpoche during a Chenrezig Initiation, December 23, 1987.

Chapter 15

1. Santideva, *Bodhisattva's Way of Life*, 63.
2. Harper Lee, *To Kill a Mockingbird* (New York: Popular Library, 1988), 30.
3. Santideva, *Bodhisattva's Way of Life*, 74.

4. Reinhold Niebuhr, *The Essential Reinhold Niebuhr: Selected Essays and Addresses*, ed. Robert McAfee Brown (New Haven, CT: Yale University Press, 1986), 251.
5. Dalai Lama, *The Good Heart*, 50.
6. Personal notes of teachings of Lama Thubten Zopa Rinpoche, Kopan Monastery, December 1987.
7. Alcoholics Anonymous, *Big Book*, 4th ed. (New York: AA World Services, 2001), 67.
8. Ibid., 66–67.
9. Santideva, *Bodhisattva's Way of Life*, 62.

Chapter 16

1. Santideva, *Bodhisattva's Way of Life*, 39.
2. Louis J. Puhl, S.J., trans., *The Spiritual Exercises of St. Ignatius* (Chicago: Loyola University Press, 1952), 12.

Chapter 17

1. Williams, *Tokens of Trust*, 6.
2. Thubten Yeshe, *Silent Mind Holy Mind* (London: Wisdom, 1978), 33.
3. Johannes Baptist Metz, *Poverty of Spirit* (Mahwah, NJ: Paulist Press, 1968), 21.

Chapter 18

1. Lama Yeshe, *Introduction to Tantra*, 42.
2. Lama Thubten Zopa Rinpoche, *Tara the Liberator* (Boston: Wisdom Publications, 1988), 14.
3. Joseph Ratzinger, *The Open Circle: The Meaning of Christian Brotherhood* (Lanham, MD: Sheed and Ward, 1966), 78.
4. Lama Yeshe, *Introduction to Tantra*, 129.
5. Nathan Katz, "From JUBU to OJ," in Kasimow, Keenan, and Keenan, *Beside Still Waters*, 43.

Chapter 20

1. St. Augustine, Sermon 8, On the Third Commandment, quoted in Martin Laird, *Into the Silent Land: A Guide to the Christian Practice of Contemplation* (Oxford: Oxford University Press, 2006), 52.

2. Wallace, *Mind in the Balance*, 45.
3. Thich Nhat Hanh, *Living Buddha, Living Christ* (New York: Riverhead Books, 1995), 16.
4. Ibid., 14.
5. Wallace, *Mind in the Balance*, 34.
6. Viktor Emil Frankl, *Man's Search for Meaning* (Clearwater, FL: Touchstone Books, 1970), ix.
7. Britta K. Hölzel, James Carmody, Mark Vangel, Christina Congleton, Sita M. Yerramsetti, Tim Gard, and Sara W. Lazar, "Mindfulness Practice Leads to Increases in Regional Brain Gray Matter Density," *Psychiatry Research: Neuroimaging* 191:36–43 (January 30, 2011).

Chapter 21

1. Nhat Hanh, *Living Buddha, Living Christ*, 90–91.
2. Michael Harter, S.J., ed., *Hearts on Fire: Praying with Jesuits* (St. Louis: Institute of Jesuit Sources, 1993), 84.
3. Conrad De Meester, *With Empty Hands: The Message of St. Therese of Lisieux* (Continuum International Publishing Group 2002), 74.
4. Carl J. Arico, *A Taste of Silence: A Guide to the Fundamentals of Centering Prayer* (Continuum International Publishing Group 1999), 152.
5. Wallace, *Mind in the Balance*, 76, quoting Saint Gregory Palamas, "In Defense of Those Who Devoutly Practice a Life of Stillness," in *The Philokalia: The Complete Text*, trans. G. E. H. Palmer, Philip Sherrard, and Kallistos Ware (London: Faber and Faber, 1995), IV:334.
6. Wallace, *Mind in the Balance*, 76, quoting Igumen Chariton of Valamo, *The Art of Prayer*, trans. E. Kadloubovsky and E. Palmer (London: Faber and Faber 1966), 183.
7. Wallace, *Mind in the Balance*, 77.
8. Karma Chagme, *A Spacious Path to Freedom: Practical Instructions on the Union of Mahamudra and Atiyoga* (Ithaca, NY: Snow Lion, 1998), 80.
9. Laird, *Into the Silent Land*, 92.
10. Wallace, *Mind in the Balance*, 94.
11. Laird, *Into the Silent Land*, 16.
12. Ibid., 20.
13. Wallace, *Mind in the Balance*, 75, quoting Heychios, "On Watchfulness and Holiness," in *The Philokalia*, I:vs.5.